More Praise for
Untangling Self

"Olendzki has done it again. In this volume he manages to make difficult teachings accessible, but without losing the challenge posed to us by the Buddhist understanding of the self. His style is even a bit deceptive, writing about profound matters in a nearly conversational voice. This book is essential to all of us who continue to puzzle over the Buddhist formulation of the self."

—Paul Fulton, coauthor and coeditor
of *Mindfulness and Psychotherapy*

"A rare gem. Wise and deeply rooted in the original Buddhist texts, *Untangling Self* is accessible and compelling, a roadmap for release from personal and societal suffering and a guide to a deeper understanding of mindfulness."

—Susan M. Pollak, MTS, EdD,
President of the Institute for Meditation and Psychotherapy

"Olendzki's perspective on Buddhist teachings carries the freshness of science and the fragrance of the Pali tradition. His voice is natural, enabling the words to reach in and touch the reader, offering both challenge and inspiration."

—Gregory Kramer, meditation teacher
and author of *Insight Dialogue*

Untangling Self

A Buddhist Investigation
of Who We Really Are

ANDREW OLENDZKI

Wisdom Publications
199 Elm Street
Somerville, MA 02144 USA
wisdomexperience.org

Library of Congress Cataloging-in-Publication Data
Names: Olendzki, Andrew, author.
Title: Untangling self : a Buddhist investigation of who we really are /
   Andrew Olendzki.
Description: Somerville, MA : Wisdom Publications, 2016. | Includes
   bibliographical references and index.
Identifiers: LCCN 2016011995 (print) | LCCN 2016040683 (ebook) | ISBN
   9781614293002 (pbk. : alk. paper) | ISBN 1614293007 (pbk.) | ISBN
   9781614293217 () | ISBN 161429321X ()
Subjects: LCSH: Buddhism—Psychology. | Buddhist ethics.
Classification: LCC BQ4570.P76 O45 2016 (print) | LCC BQ4570.P76 (ebook) |
   DDC 294.3/422—dc23
LC record available at https://lccn.loc.gov/2016011995

ISBN 978-1-61429-300-2   ebook ISBN 978-1-61429-321-7

25 24 23 22 21
6 5 4 3 2

Cover design by Philip Pascuzzo.
Interior design by Gopa & Ted2, Inc. Set in Garamond Premier Pro 11.6/15.8.

Contents

Publisher's Acknowledgment

The publisher gratefully acknowledges the generous contribution of the Hershey Family Foundation toward the publication of this book.

Introduction:
The Challenge of Nonself

Tangled within, tangled without;
People are tangled in tangles.
And so I ask you, Gotama—
"Who can untangle this tangle?"

A wise one of stable virtue,
Developing mind and wisdom,
A prudent and ardent person—
They can untangle this tangle.[1]

The scientific enterprise has looked closely at the world around us for several centuries now, using ever-more-powerful tools and interpretive models to do so, and it has a lot of things pretty well figured out. Profound mysteries remain at the frontiers of knowledge, of course, and perhaps one of the things we have learned is that such unknowns may always exist. But there is not much in the midsection of the universe we inhabit, between the very smallest and very largest levels of scale, about which we do not have a pretty good working knowledge. Yet for all this impressive accumulation, we know very little about the knowers of this knowledge. That is to say, we still do not know ourselves very well.

It has been both easier and more useful to look outward rather than inward, for the material world is quite obedient to natural laws and learning to exploit these laws has been rewarded with many practical advantages. But the time has come to turn our instruments on ourselves in earnest in an effort to understand the greatest mystery of all. Who are we? What is the self? What is this phenomenon that stands in the center of everything trying to understand it all?

We are fortunate to live in a time when so much is being learned about the mind and the brain, when consciousness itself is a favored topic of focused investigation, and when experimental tools and techniques for investigating the subject are evolving so dramatically. Hardly a week goes by without a significant new insight into the mind emerging from researchers and theorists around the globe. Under the influence of dramatic advances in the modern understanding of mind, brain, and behavior, we are witnessing a systematic deconstruction of the idea of the self as an essential entity. It is being redefined as a bundle of socially influenced narratives and behavioral patterns that has emerged gradually during early development and undergoes continual modification as experience unfolds. This is familiar territory for Buddhists, who have been making a similar point for some time now.

The reason the self causes difficulty is that it is simultaneously so intuitively obvious and such a confused idea. Buddhists consider it a folk belief, a superstition, a conceptual reflex, a linguistic habit, a mistaken assumption, a fuzzy idea, a mirage. This is why the Buddha stayed away from it as much as possible, even remaining silent when pressed upon the subject. To say the self does not exist is as problematic as saying it does exist, because the whole notion of self is flawed to the bone. So much so, in fact, that the burden of proof to explain what they mean by it should be upon those who use the notion of self, rather than on those who would question its existence. Like the flatness of the earth or the solidity of the table, it has utility at a certain level of scale—socially, linguistically, legally—but thoroughly breaks down when examined with closer scrutiny.

Long ago we stopped answering the question of why it rains with the use of an agent noun. Once, perhaps, the rain god made it rain, or God made it rain. Surely now most people will allow that rain occurs when certain conditions (temperature, humidity, etc.) come together in a particular combination. When those conditions no longer prevail, the rain stops. It does not *go* anywhere, it just no longer happens. Every single thing in the natural world occurs in the same way. When certain factors come together in certain ways, certain things happen. When those factors change, those things dissipate and other things happen. There is no intrinsic identity in anything. There are only the labels we decide upon to refer to things: clouds, raindrops, puddles. All persons, places, and things are merely names that we give to certain patterns we call out from the incessant flux of interdependent natural events.

Why are human beings different than this? How could humans possibly be anything other than a natural part of the natural world? Surely "Joe" is just something that occurs when conditions come together in certain ways, and Joe no longer occurs when those conditions change enough. Sometimes, when certain things are happening, Joe is a nice guy; at other times, when other things are happening, Joe can be a real jerk. Under some conditions Joe is living; when the conditions supporting Joe's life no longer occur, Joe will no longer be living. He is not the sort of thing that can *go* somewhere else (to heaven or to another body, for example), except perhaps in the most abstract sense of the recycling of his constituent components. All this is as natural as a rainstorm in the summer.

Many writers have been gently but relentlessly dismantling the assumed notion of self while chronicling the progress of cognitive neuroscience and related fields over the previous several decades. One example is Bruce Hood's *The Self Illusion*. Undermining our common presumptions of unity, coherence, stability, agency, and the ever-popular homunculus, Hood leaves us with a simple but astonishing insight: that the self has been carved through experience by the environment it inhabits, and particularly by the other selves (or self illusions) that surround it. "You only exist as a pattern made up of all the other things in your life that shape you," he concludes. But he reassures us, just as the Buddhists have done, "This does not mean that you do not exist at all, but rather that you exist as a combination of all the others who complete your sense of self." This is the new face of interdependence.

As gratifying as it can be to see ancient Buddhist ideas corroborated by cutting-edge neuroscience and experimental psychology, one cannot help but sense that the two approaches to understanding the self are not entirely engaged in the same enterprise. A considerable gap remains between modern and ancient perspectives on the subject, and it is naturally difficult for each to conceive the territory that lies beyond the point where its own approach leaves off. Perhaps we can come at this divide from both sides, describing it from the point of view of each of the traditions in turn.

The remarkable successes of scientific research and theorizing come from the powerful methodologies of science, one of which is to engage in a close study of an object from a third-person or objective perspective. Instead of merely accepting traditionally preserved viewpoints without question, or theorizing from abstract principles by deduction, science examines an object carefully, records its properties and functions, and then induces general explanatory principles from the evidence at hand. This approach has worked well for anything that can be placed under a microscope or pointed to with a telescope, both literally and figuratively speaking. As we bring this approach to the study of ourselves, we notice that for the most part the modern study of mind involves the study of other people's minds. We look at other people's behavior in various controlled situations, we scan other people's brains in our imaging devices, and we dissect, probe, and stimulate other people's neurons. The modern study of the self is essentially a third-person enterprise, and thus it follows in the mold of all previous scientific research.

But it seems increasingly apparent that consciousness is something not to be sufficiently comprehended this way. We can study the structure and function of the brain's neurons, transmitters, and other components, and we can study the actions and reactions of behavior, but the states in between, the subjective phenomenology of human experience, seem fundamentally inaccessible to existing methods of inquiry. There is no instrument that can measure what it feels like to have an experience, there is no data set that can adequately record the nuances of a felt sensation, there is no theorem that can encompass the many idiosyncrasies of a unique human being.

What is most troubling about this situation is that it may not simply be a matter of developing the next generation of gadgetry or designing some brilliant new laboratory experiment. It may be that no third-person explanation can ever address the phenomenon of selfhood, insofar as it will always be imbedded in a first-person perspective. This is now a philosophical problem rather than a scientific one. There may still be plenty of ways we might more and more adequately describe the workings of the mind, body, and behavior, but it may also be true that something essential to understanding the self will remain forever out of reach to this kind of explanation. No matter how good the microscope or telescope, such instruments can never be turned directly upon the one gazing into the eyepiece.

Let's now look at how the problem presents itself from the Buddhist perspective. According to classical Buddhist thought, self is a view. As such it is a product of the aggregate of perception (*saññā*). Perception is the function of the mind that creates meaning, that paints a picture or constructs a model of what is going on every moment. It does so by creating signs (*nimitta*) or thoughts (*vitakka*) or concepts (*paññatti*) or views (*diṭṭhi*)—symbols of some sort to represent what it is that is seen with the eye, heard with the ear, smelled with the nose, tasted with the tongue, touched with the body, or thought with the mind. One image offered in the early texts is of a carpenter placing a mark on the end of a piece of lumber, so he can easily identify its type, length, quality, etc. The view of self (*sakkāya-diṭṭhi*) is a constructed illusion, as are all of our perceptions.

The stream of perceptions, flowing along with the stream of consciousness, provides an ongoing interpretation of experience, moment after moment, as each episode of cognition is enacted and then fades away. As with every other aspect of the mind and body, perception is an event that occurs rather than a thing that exists, and as such individual views of what is happening arise and vanish one after another in rapid succession and have no enduring substance. Yet just as with the stream of consciousness, such fleeting images are patched together in our minds like a filmstrip to create a relatively stable and coherent perceptual narrative.

Ultimately the entire scientific enterprise is one of creating and refining conceptual models of the world we inhabit. It is about constructing ever more accurate and useful perceptions. The collective enterprise of furthering the subtlety and explanatory power of these models yields immense practical benefits and can also give rise to profound intellectual and aesthetic satisfaction. The progress of human understanding is indeed impressive, and it has provided us with the means of radically shaping our world.

Buddhists are not particularly interested in this agenda. There is nothing wrong with coming up with more and more sophisticated ways of conceptually representing the world, and certainly it is better to have accurate views than distorted views, but this is not really where the action is. Perception is not primarily responsible for the arising of suffering, and it plays only a supporting role in the cessation of suffering. It is within the aggregate of *sankhāra*, of emotional, volitional, and behavioral formations, that both the causes and solutions to suffering are to be found. The content of perception is not nearly as important as the matter of how we respond to it. The Buddha was thus addressing a very different issue than the contemporary theoretical scientist.

The five aggregates (*khandha*) are always coarising and working together to forge who we are and what we do. The materiality (*rūpa*) of the four great elements (solid, liquid, gas, heat) making up the body and the environment it inhabits is foundational, as is consciousness (*viññāna*), which provides the basic function of knowing or awareness of an object. These are augmented by perception (*saññā*) and feeling tone (*vedanā*), which create a sense of what is happening and how it feels to us—pleasant or painful. The fifth aggregate (*sankhāra*) involves our emotional response to the object of the moment, the liking or not liking of it, the wanting or not wanting it, and a whole range of other possible responses toward what we experience. We never just notice an object, we *engage* with it emotionally.

Such engagement with experience is intrinsically immediate and personal. Not personal in the sense of our narrative self, which is a story woven by perception, but in the most intimate and existential sense of the word personal. The self is created by our emotional responses as they unfold each moment: when we crave for an object of experience, then "the person who" wants it is constructed; when we generate aversion toward an object, then "the person who" hates it comes into existence. The person we are each moment is forged by these emotional responses, which is why they are so much more immediate and constitutive of identity than are perceptions. What we think is a part of it, but what we do and have done is more fundamental to who we are and what we will do.

Since perceptions and emotions arise and pass away interdependently, they often influence and shape one another. But it matters little whether you hate someone because they hurt your feelings, or because you think they are a threat, or maybe simply because they are called Joe—it is the hating as an emotional response that causes suffering for yourself and those around you. Often enough perception simply offers a rationale for an emotion that has its real origin in the unexamined depths of the unconscious.

In the Buddhist model, therefore, refining perception is not itself going to be transformative. If perception can help guide and mold our emotional responses, such as occurs when certain phrases are used to help develop loving kindness for all beings ("May they be happy, safe, and healthy"), that is a good thing. But in this case it is the emotion of kindness itself that is unraveling the bonds of suffering, with perception of "beings" being "happy" playing only an auxiliary role.

The consequence of this insight is that third-person scientific knowledge is not in itself going to get underneath what is most important to modifying human behavior. As Socrates says in the *Phaedo*, the philosopher's explanation of how the bones and sinews bind his body together can never explain why he has chosen to drink the hemlock rather than flee to Megara. Or, as the Buddha says to Mālunkyāputta, knowing who shot the arrow, or from what bird the feathers are made, will not contribute to the urgent task of pulling it out and healing the wound.

Wisdom in Buddhist thought is not the forging of proper conceptual ideas as much as it is an unbinding of the mind from the clutches of desire. The reason insight into nonself is transformative is not because it counters the mistaken ideas of self by providing a better conceptual model (though it does this too) but because it loosens the emotional bonds of clinging—clinging to sense desires, clinging to views, clinging to conventions, clinging to self. This will always be a first-person experience, accessed through the first-person technology of moral action (*sīla*), mental development (*samādhi*), and direct insight (*paññā*). As the Kālāmas are told, listening to teachers will only take you so far; one must know *for oneself* what is harmful and then abandon it in order for such knowledge to be transformational. This is a much more difficult challenge.

There is an assumption somewhere within us that says if only we can understand what is happening, everything will be all right. Yet an argument might be made that even as we are understanding more and more about how our universe operates, we are at the same time getting deeper and deeper into trouble. Our knowledge is still under the thrall of greed, hatred, and delusion, the three primary afflictive emotions identified in the Buddhist tradition. What is called for is not more conceptual understanding but greater emotional maturity, which can only come from better self-knowledge.

We know, for example, in increasing detail how economic, political, and social systems that are in place are contributing to the dramatic degradation of the global environment. We don't have a clue, however, about how to help people disengage from the root instincts that are causing this: (a) to get more of what one wants whenever possible and at whatever cost to others (=greed); (b) to hurt anything or kill anyone who stands in the way of this or who otherwise is seen as posing a threat (=hatred); (c) to be complacent and generally not know or not care about what is happening beyond the scope of one's own immediate self (=delusion). In short we understand increasingly well the harm we are causing, but we have very little understanding of how to prevent ourselves from doing it.

Many people in many fields are contributing to this larger, more important project. Dismantling the essential self is a good start, and preferably doing so in ways that are not foreign to the modern reader. Just as Mindfulness-Based Stress Reduction was able to infiltrate the mainstream medical profession to make Buddhist meditation practices more accessible to all, perhaps a new wave of psychologists, neuroscientists, and philosophers can help penetrate the defenses of the inviolable autonomous self and allow greater access to the healing powers of Buddhist wisdom. This in turn might help loosen some of the bonds preventing the evolution of a more altruistic species and contribute to a lessening of suffering and a general elevation of well-being. The self, as conventionally understood, may turn out to be more trouble than it is worth, and we all may well be better off without it.

1 Understanding the Buddha

Then with the gleaming of the night,
Close to the rising of the sun,
All my craving simply dried up
As I sat there with my legs crossed.[2]

THE RADICAL BUDDHA

Every Buddha image we see reflects such calm, amused acceptance, it is not easy to appreciate just how radical a figure Siddhartha Gotama Buddha really was. Yet when we look closely at the ways he acted in the world he inhabited, and at the teachings he left behind for us all to follow, I think it fair to say the Buddha was one of the more radical humans ever to have walked the earth.

The word *radical*, according to a pocket dictionary at hand, most simply means "favoring fundamental change." This is a surprising definition, but it certainly suits the Buddha well. The first really radical thing the Buddha did was walk away from a very comfortable life as prince and heir-apparent of an admittedly minor kingdom. This is not unheard of, but it was remarkable for not having been precipitated by the death of a loved one, a sudden illness, a political reversal, or by some other disruptive event. The counterculture calling him was itself rather radical, espousing as it did the value of giving up all possessions, severing all social ties, and voluntarily taking up an uncomfortable lifestyle.

He soon mastered the yogic meditative techniques of the day, and was offered an esteemed position as coleader of not one but two meditation groups. Turning away from a promising career as a meditation teacher, which also would have involved a lot of time spent in a state of "pleasant abiding here and now," was the second radical thing done by the Buddha. In both cases he aligned himself with fundamental change rather than acquiescing to the status quo.

Next he took up extreme ascetic practices, and among other things starved himself to within an inch of his life. The radical part, however, is that here too he turned away from these practices when he realized for himself they were not effective in purifying his mind. In the context of the ascetic groups with whom he lived this was seen as a complete failure, and he was ridiculed by his associates when he reverted to a life of luxury by eating more than a grain of rice a day. The "middle path" lifestyle he then settled upon and sustained for the duration of his life was itself a courageous resolution of the extremes of indulgence and asceticism, and it would have struck both his aristocratic kindred and his wanderer compatriots as radical.

Things got exponentially more radical, however, when he declared the community he founded to be uncompromisingly without caste distinction, and when he offered equal (though parallel) regard for women. To insist that former Brahmins must eat and drink beside former untouchables, and that women were made up of the same interdependent aggregates, sense bases, and elements as men, and were therefore equally capable of wisdom and awakening, was favoring a most radical change in the social order of the day.

But it is the Buddha's teachings that most pushed back against the received wisdom of the generations and that continue to challenge us today. To say not that *some* things change but that *all* things change, and that there is no stability anywhere, was and remains a radical thing to say. To then go on to apply that insight not only to the world out there but to us, to our very *selves*, is about as radical as it gets. There is no true self behind the apparent self, no large self embracing the small self, no universal self permeating and enveloping the personal self—there is just no such self at all. The self is a beautiful idea, but alas, it is a mistaken idea. Whatever self there is shifts and changes, arises and falls away, is born and dies, just like everything else in this changing universe.

It is also radical to acknowledge suffering as a noble truth, given the extent to which humans go to cover over or deny it. Others have said that this life is hard but escape from hardship is forthcoming in the next life, or that life's hardship is a test that can be passed successfully to reap lasting reward, or that one can call upon divine help for coping with the challenges. Unlike these the Buddha accepted as a fundamental truth that pain is an inevitable and inescapable component of the human condition, and that each of us must face this in the intimacy of our own experience.

But he also declared that suffering has its causes within the natural world and can thus be addressed with the natural means at hand. Suffering is caused by resistance to pain and by attachment to pleasure, resulting in a nonalignment with the change that is so fundamental to the natural order. It is radically empowering to say that suffering is caused by human maladaptation to the way things are, and that it can thus be eliminated by a psychological adjustment—by evolving our understanding and learning to respond differently.

If we can accomplish this, as the Buddha did, then we are capable of attaining a state of radical well-being. It is possible to hold oneself in this very world, with all its challenges, in such a way that we are neither seduced into addiction by pleasure nor frightened into loathing by pain, and all mental states are characterized by an attitude of generosity, kindness, compassion, joy for the well-being of others, and a deep, penetrating wisdom that sees all things just as they are.

For those of us living in today's world, even if we fall short of this most compelling ideal, the Buddha offers the transformative insight that the world we inhabit is made and ruled by our own minds. Every problem we face as a species gradually despoiling its habitat is caused by our own greed, hatred, and delusion, and therefore it can be challenged and overcome by purifying our own minds of these toxins.

I think the Buddha smiles slightly as he looks upon all this with benevolent amusement because he realizes we are all capable of inhabiting a healthy world in profound happiness. We need only "favor fundamental change" and discover thereby the most radical thing of all—freedom.

A MODEST AWAKENING

The earth shook at dawn and the devas rejoiced that morning long ago when the wanderer Gotama attained *nirvana* by "waking up" under the Bodhi tree to become the Buddha. The sky rained flowers out of season and the devas lamented forty-five years later, as the Buddha passed away between twin Sal trees in Kusinara in what has come to be called the *parinirvana*. These were two very different events that, I believe, require entirely different explanations.

The first was a psychological event, focusing on extraordinary changes in the way experience gets constructed by the mind as it operates in the world; the second was a metaphysical event, having to do with issues of rebirth, postmortem consciousness, and the emerging theology of a growing religious movement. In most popular discussions of awakening, however, the distinction between them gets blurred, which naturally leads to some confusion.

In the years between these two events, as the Buddha walked from town to village along the Ganges valley, people would come to him wanting to know what happened to him under that tree, and how they too might be able to accomplish the same feat. He talked about it in terms of a thorough psychological transformation. Before the moment of awakening his mind constructed suffering in the same way the rest of us do, forged in the fires of craving, but in the moment afterward his mind was dramatically purified of all unwholesome or unskillful states.

All the emotions rooted in greed, hatred, and delusion were cut off, uprooted, annihilated, dried up, extinguished, withdrawn, and otherwise abandoned once and for all, such that it was no longer possible for them to manifest in his experience. He speaks of it as finding peace, becoming cool, reaching safety, putting down the burden, attaining liberation, and he uses a wide range of similar imagery to express the final, irreversible cessation of suffering. And he continued to live for the duration of his natural life as any other man might—eating, sleeping, talking, and meditating—though as one who experiences an unshakable sense of well-being in the face of any and all conditions.

At the end of his life he says to his loyal attendant Ananda: "Since whatever is born, become, compounded is subject to decay, how could it be that my body should not pass away?" Soon after, when his body had been respectfully cleaned, wrapped, and cremated, and the ashes distributed equitably, the question inevitably arose: How are we to understand what has just happened? What has become of our Teacher? It is not appropriate to say the Buddha had gone to another realm, since he clearly said he had escaped this entire world system and would not be reborn in any of its various destinations. Neither is it fitting to say he died, since he also declared he had defeated Mara, the lord of death, and had attained the Deathless. All other available options, encompassing subtle variations on the theme of existence and nonexistence, perception and nonperception, seem also to have been considered and excluded, resulting in a profound and lasting paradox.

When asked earlier what happens to an awakened person after death, the Teacher famously remained silent. When pressed for an explanation, he suggested things like: it is a wrongly posed question; no one could understand the answer; the means of expressing what happens just do not exist; or the issue is entirely irrelevant. We have our hands full dealing with experience as it presents itself each moment, so trying to understand conceptually what is clearly beyond common experience is not a worthwhile use of the precious time remaining to us. Just let go of speculative views on the subject, focus skillfully on what is arising and passing away in direct experience, and you may see for yourself someday.

Of course human nature being what it is, very few are capable of finding this a satisfactory answer. Splendid and nuanced treatments

of the subject are to be found in Sanskrit sutras, Tibetan philosophical treatises, and in the rich visual imagery of East Asian art. However,
since so many of the explanations of how to understand the *parinirvana*
tend toward the cosmological, pointing quite beyond verifiable direct
experience, I worry that his life's teaching about *nirvana* as an accessible psychological transformation in this life has become overshadowed
and even undervalued. This is not about calling these later resolutions
of the paradox into question, but rather of excavating and recovering a
more modest view of *nirvana* from that sliver of Buddhist tradition laid
down during his lifetime.

What if the *nirvana* experienced by the Buddha in Bodhgaya turns
out to be something considerably less magnificent than that of later
mythic tradition, yet at the same time, by virtue of it being actually
attainable by ordinary folk, something of unparalleled value?

As a psychological transformation the Buddha spoke of learning how
to be deeply happy, right here and now, no matter what circumstances
we are facing. Even the existential challenges of our own impending illness, aging, and death can be encompassed with a wisdom that
acknowledges all things change, accepts there is no essence underlying
it all, and is able nevertheless to meet each moment without clinging to
anything in the world.

The early texts tell us that the Buddha was able to lead many, many
people—man and woman, Brahmin and outcaste, aristocrat and mer-
chant, ordained and layperson—to a state of no longer struggling with
the human condition. I really do not know what happens to such a person when they die, any more than I know what became of the Buddha. Somehow that seems less relevant than the remarkable prospect
of attaining profound well-being simply by understanding the causes of
suffering in lived experience, and managing to unravel those causes each
moment as life unfolds.

The Buddha's own description of his midlife transformation is compelling in its simplicity and immediacy:

Indeed the sage who's fully quenched
Rests at ease in every way;
No sense desire adheres to one
Whose fires have cooled, deprived of fuel.
All attachments have been severed,
The heart's been led away from pain;
Tranquil, one rests with utmost ease,
The mind has found its way to peace.[3]

THE OTHER DUKKHA

One of the more difficult parts of the Buddha's story to reconcile with modern sensibilities is the fact that he left home, abandoning his wife and newborn son, to wander forth into the wilderness as a spiritual seeker. The interpretation of this fact among the general public tends to be that it was a selfish act, insofar as it was oriented toward his own emancipation from the bonds of human limitation.

I would like to offer an alternative perspective on the matter, one suggested by Ashvaghosha's treatment of the episode in his marvelous later Sanskrit poem *Buddhacarita*. He seems to identify the Buddha's motivation as growing from a heightened sensitivity to the situation of others, and I think in doing so he lays out a basis upon which modern Engaged Buddhism can be solidly built. Here are two stanzas of the poem that set the tone, as translated by Patrick Olivelle:

But when a man happens to see
someone who is old, sick, or dead
and remains at ease, unperturbed,
he's the same as a senseless man.
For when one tree is stripped
of its flowers or fruits;
or when it's cut down or falls,
another tree does not grieve.[4]

To be sentient, suggests Ashvaghosha, is to be moved by the misfortune of others. From this point of view, it would have been selfish of Siddhartha to remain embedded in a life of luxury, and it was an act of heroism for him to sacrifice that comfort to wander forth seeking a cure to suffering which could then be shared with all. The critical shift from narcissism to altruism comes from regarding the prince as not so much terrified of his own impending doom as responding sympathetically to the suffering he saw others encountering.

In contemporary dialogue the first noble truth is usually interpreted to mean that each of us individually must experience the disappointment of not getting what we want or of having to contend with what we don't want. Suffering also refers to the existential bummer of having to endure old age, illness, and death, but again the emphasis is upon how this impinges on our own personal happiness. But I think *dukkha* has always referred at least equally—and possibly even mostly—to the suffering our actions inflict upon others.

When the resource I consume runs out and I am left wanting more, there is indeed some moment of personal psychological disappointment before I successfully grasp for another helping. But, unseen by me, there is also a price being paid somewhere by someone struggling to provide that resource, and he or she may not be doing so freely, safely, or fairly. And when I turn away from reports of others in pain or need, because paying attention to the details of their situation is a source of unpleasant feelings for me, there is a moment of being uncomfortable before I am able to fasten upon something more gratifying. But the suffering of the other remains, and it only deepens from my inattention.

The cause of suffering is desire, manifesting in its two opposite forms of greed and hatred. Each of these are mental states that flash briefly, though repeatedly, through the mind as one makes decisions and then acts on those decisions. The actions rooted in greed and hatred then reverberate out through a vast network of cause and effect, and I think the noble truth of suffering is broad enough to include both the momentary impulse of the intention and the lasting harm the deeds they generate can do to others. The prince Siddhartha awoke to the realization that he was living in a bubble, and possibly also to the fact that it was being carried on the backs of other living creatures who were suffering as a result. The spark for this awakening was empathy toward others, for example as he watched a plowman at work:

> Clumps of grass dug up by the plow littered the earth,
> covered with tiny dead creatures, insects and worms;
> as he beheld the earth with all these strewn about,
> he grieved greatly, as if a kinsman had been killed.
> Seeing the men plowing the fields, their bodies discolored
> by the wind, the dust, the scorching rays of the sun,
> oxen wearied by the toil of pulling the plows,
> great compassion overwhelmed that great noble man.[5]

What made him unique was his inability to acquiesce to his own personal comfort when surrounded by others who were suffering. As the prince says to a friend trying to talk him into remaining in the palace:

> O how steady and strong your mind must be
> that you see substance in fleeting pleasures,
> that, seeing these creatures on the path of death,
> you are attached to sensual pleasures
> in the midst of the most frightful dangers.
> I, however, am timid, much perturbed,
> as I think of the dangers
> of old age, sickness, and death;
> I find no peace or content, much less joy,
> seeing the world with fire as if ablaze.[6]

Dukkha does not only mean that we feel unhappy some of the time. It also means that many of the things we do cause other people to suffer. When actions (or inactions) are tainted with various shades of greed, hatred, and delusion, they cause real harm. In a thoroughly interdependent world, one's own happiness cannot successfully be built upon the suffering of others. This is the realization that turned the prince away from his own gratification to face in a new direction, and it may well be the insight that launches the new Buddhism in an untraditionally outward trajectory.

From the beginning Buddhists have had concern for the welfare of others, and this accelerated with the later impulse of grounding personal practice in the vow to benefit all sentient beings. Yet this seemed to have more to do with purifying the front end of action, its motivation or intention, rather than engaging directly with the back end of action, the harm already inflicted upon the world by a toxic mind. In our time Buddhists are increasingly interested in alleviating suffering more directly, envisioning a sustained practice of engaged activity in service to others.

It is entirely appropriate to examine in our own moment-to-moment experience how craving and aversion manifest in personal psychological suffering. It is also important to follow that strand out through the interdependent karmic relationships in which each such moment is entangled, to see how our desire is affecting everyone and everything around us. We thereby practice the full range of the second noble truth, understanding the causes of suffering. And to practice both aspects of the third noble truth, the cessation of that suffering, we must work to extinguish not only the internal source of the craving in our own minds but also the external consequences of that craving in the world we have created.

A PROTESTANT BUDDHISM

"Protestant Buddhism" is a label that has been applied to certain progressive elements in the Theravada tradition, first in Sri Lanka in the nineteenth century, and more recently to modernist Buddhism in this country and around the globe. It is sometimes used as a pejorative, to the extent the enterprise is regarded as tainted with orientalist and colonialist attitudes and the move by modern, progressive Buddhists to "improve upon" traditional forms of Buddhism. Another point against it is its tendency to downplay or even marginalize the role of the ordained Sangha.

Yet there is also much to be said in favor of modernist trends in contemporary Buddhism, and I wonder if we might find a way of rehabilitating Protestant Buddhism to the satisfaction of its critics. A crucial first step in the process is to recognize that new forms of Buddhism, at their best, are based upon creative ways of synthesizing meaning rather than upon criticizing the beliefs or practices of others. In other words while it is not okay to say others have got it wrong and this is the right way of looking at things, it is entirely appropriate (even natural) to say, "Here is an interesting new way of understanding things that I find particularly intriguing and meaningful."

Let's look at some of the parallels. In ancient India the Brahmins held specialized sacred knowledge of the Vedic hymns and were the only ones qualified to perform the rituals needed for the well-being of the population. The entire Shramana movement was a rebellion against this privileged information, and the Buddha, like other wandering ascetics, taught that anyone can gain direct access to spiritual wisdom by practicing meditation and understanding the Dhamma for themselves. This is much like the Protestants in Europe bypassing the Church and empowering people to study the Bible for themselves to forge their own meaning from it directly.

Over twenty-five centuries an orthodox Theravada establishment grew and flourished in many Buddhist countries, built upon a preservation of the Pali texts and their explication in commentaries such as those by Buddhaghosa. The monks (and nuns?) had direct access to the teachings through the study of Pali and the practice of meditation, while the laity was cast in a supporting role of sustaining the monastics and practicing generosity and ethical behavior. In the early twentieth century some Burmese teachers encouraged householders to practice meditation intensively on ten-day retreats, thus making the insights deriving from such practice directly available to them. This is one of the forms in which Theravada Buddhism was exported from Asia, and such regular meditation practice became popular among convert Buddhists in America and elsewhere in the West.

Another development that gained momentum over the course of the twentieth century was the study of Buddhist texts and languages, including the complete translation of the Pali canon. Good editions of these texts are now readily available to all in the English-speaking world, and even tools for learning Pali are within easy reach. While we have not quite arrived at the point of finding a copy of the *Dhammapada* in one's hotel room drawer, certainly almost every bookstore carries some selection of primary Buddhist texts, with many freely available on the internet. And people are reading them.

One of the more foundational insights of Buddhism, aligning it with the postmodern world view, is that a world of meaning is constructed anew each moment by each individual mind/body organism. The world is not "out there" but is constructed "in this fathom-long body." As information flows into the various sense doors, mediated by the structures of our sensory apparatus and the functions of our mental aggregates, views form about who we are and what sort of environment we inhabit. These views are often mistaken—distorted by delusion, clouded by defilements, beset with ignorance—but we do the best we can each moment to gradually clarify and deepen our understanding. The process is aided by both hearing or reading the Dhamma and investigating its meaning in personal meditative experience.

This being the case, having direct access to the teachings of the Buddha, and being encouraged and supported in the regular practice of meditation, can only be a good thing. Even if we get it wrong once in a while, there may be greater value in actively inquiring into the meaning of the Dhamma at every opportunity than in passively accepting a tradition in whatever form it has been handed down to us by the previous generation. How many times has the Buddha said, "Listen carefully, and

I will speak . . . ," and how many times do we find the phrase "Here are the roots of trees. Meditate!"?

Care must be taken to avoid the pitfalls. We are not necessarily better at understanding these teachings than all the Buddhists before us just because we are moderns or humanists or typing on keyboards. We cannot assume that the troubling bits, about miracles, rebirth, and hell realms, for example, must not be "true" and that we, of course, know better. It is possible to hold the greatest respect for all those who think differently than ourselves, for all those who construct their own meaning of these teachings differently that we do, and simply say at some point that we do not share that way of seeing things. There is a huge difference between thinking differently from another and considering the other to be mistaken.

So by all means let us keep reading the texts very carefully, and see how creatively and meaningfully we can allow the teachings they contain to guide the way we live our lives and shape our world. Let's also engage in the careful investigation of experience, moment by moment, and allow the insights gained to inform and inspire our understanding. As part of this practice, let us be closely watchful over our own attitudes to ensure that toxins such as pride, intolerance, or prejudice about other opinions do not spill out and reveal how much work still must be done. And, let's continue to honor and learn from the Elders, as they have much to contribute to this process.

2 Mindfulness and Meditation

Engage with the Buddha's teaching!
One who does so has no regrets.[7]

FINDING THE CENTER

Imagine you walk into an small empty room that is totally dark, and you are asked to locate its center point. How might you proceed? Unable to use the sense of sight you might begin by going around the room with one hand on the wall, exploring the perimeter. Once you've turned the corner four times, you can be fairly sure you are more or less back where you started.

Next you might push off boldly from one wall and traverse the whole room until you crash into the opposite wall. Bouncing back and forth between these two walls, you would eventually get a sense of the midpoint between them. Thus oriented, you might then turn ninety degrees and shuffle between the other two walls along this centerline until you find what appears to be half the distance between them.

By now you have a pretty good sense of where you are and can locate with some confidence the center of the room. Reaching up, your hand encounters a string dangling from the ceiling; pulling it, the light comes on and the darkness is dispelled.

I find this a useful metaphor for *samatha* (calming) meditation practice. In particular, it describes the process of retreating from the five hindrances to find the still, peaceful center point of the mind. Every student of meditation knows these five hindrances (*nivarana*) well. The word literally means "to cover over, obstruct, or hide," and in this application consciousness is being obstructed by sense desire, aversion, restlessness, and sluggishness (the four walls of our room), while being obscured by the darkness of doubt.

The first thing most people notice when they sit down to meditate is that the mind is restless. We are used to processing so much information, the mind has developed the habit of working quickly and is always hungry for more input. The antidote to this natural tendency is to slow down and relax both body and mind, which of course is easier said than done. The instructions found in the *Discourse on the Establishment of Mindfulness*[8] start with becoming aware of the breath and then move immediately into training yourself to tranquilize the activity of breathing.

Whether it takes a few minutes, a few days, or a few years, eventually one can learn the skill of deep relaxation. Peacefulness is a living experience that can be cultivated by holding still, letting go, and allowing oneself to settle down into the quiet depths of the mind, again and again, one moment after another. The cumulative effect of this patient perseverance is a growing sense of ease, of comfort, of gentle well-being, until . . . *bonk!* —you hit the other wall of mental sloth and torpor.

At some point all this tranquility devolves into sleepiness, laziness, or a sluggishness of mind where it seems a struggle just to remain conscious. This too is natural, and it does not mean you are doing anything wrong. Having established these two end points on a continuum, practice involves moving back and forth between them until one finds the point of equilibrium. You can get a sense when the mind is too active, at which point you let go of your attachment to the stimulant du jour and allow the mind to rest. And when you feel it getting drowsy, it is time to sit up straighter, take a deeper breath, and give yourself a little mental kick into wakefulness. Eventually, becoming familiar with both ends of this spectrum, you will find the midpoint where the mind is simultaneously tranquil and alert.

Moving perpendicularly, we then notice that the mind is drawn habitually toward those objects of experience it finds gratifying. This need not be full-on lust or the irresistible drive of addiction; more often it is a gentle inclination toward what we like. The senses revel in sensation, the mind delights in mentation, and we are usually "leaning in" to the next moment and faintly grasping after the next experience. Notice this, and softly back away from it.

In the other direction we can also observe the tendency to pull back from the things we don't like or don't want. Much of what we encounter can be experienced with a subtle sense of annoyance or dissatisfaction. "Yeah, I'm noticing the breath all right, but I don't like that pain in the back and wish it would just go away." Can we also bounce between these two walls, between the impulse to like and not like what is happening? The experience of pleasure and pain is inevitable, part of the hard wiring of the body and mind. But the wanting and not wanting that arises with these feeling tones are optional emotional responses that can be modified by conscious intention.

The midpoint between sense desire and aversion is equanimity, a state of mind that is evenly balanced. It is fully engaged with experience, but it neither favors nor opposes what is happening. We are aware of what is arising and passing away without any inclination to change it into something else. When this equanimity is coupled with a mind that is both tranquil and alert, we have found the still center of the mind. You may well have to bump into all four walls over and over in your search, but you will surely know when you find this "sweet spot"—because it feels wonderful.

The doubts that obscure ordinary mind states and keep us from this center point—doubts about whether we have the right teacher, about whether we are doing the practice correctly, and many others—are dispelled, for the moment, and all is illuminated with trust and confidence. The body feels entirely comfortable, even if gravely afflicted. The mind feels clear and powerful, even if it is normally battered by anxiety or fear. The still center of the mind is a place of universal refuge that can be accessed again and again once one learns the way there. And even if the experience vanishes as soon as it occurs, which it is very likely to do, you can retrace your steps to find it again. You may even learn how to hover there indefinitely . . .

This is not nirvana, but it is its base camp. It is a stable, peaceful refuge from which one can explore the inner landscape of experience and see things more clearly as they actually are.

MIND LIKE A MIRROR

> The mind is luminous, but it is polluted by the toxins
> dumped into it.[9]

This is a translation, updated for our times, of a well-known passage found in the early discourses of the Buddha. It has been taken by some to point toward a transpersonal consciousness that is somehow abiding below, behind, or above the consciousness arising each moment in a person's sensory or mental experience, but it does not seem to have this sense in the early literature. Rather we find the image of a pool of limpid water that, when still, can clearly reflect the nature of whatever impinges upon it. It is not a force larger than ourselves but a process taking place within ourselves, with no individualizing characteristics beyond the basic function of knowing an object. Mind is thus neither the source of light, like a shining sun—as some Hindus would have it—nor the reflected light of something greater, like the moon—as some Christians would have it—but a shimmering pool of contingent potential, capable of reflecting sun, moon, and any other object that happens to dance upon its surface. Its function is more important than its essence, and it is influenced significantly by the nature of what gets stirred into its pristine waters.

The diversity of experience comes not from consciousness itself but from the other four aggregates in the mix: an apparently infinite array of physical and mental objects; the interpretation of these by means of the symbolic language of perception; their texturing with varying shades of pleasant and unpleasant feeling tones; and both the active intentions and passive dispositions that respond each moment to the impingement of these objects with the enacting of karma. In this sense consciousness itself is like a mirror, whose only function is to reflect whatever it encounters—the content and quality of experience is provided by other mental processes. In particular it is the karma formations of the *sankhāra* aggregate that tint the experience of an object with mental states and emotional responses. Whenever we see, hear, smell, taste, touch, or think of an object, we do so with a particular attitude or emotion that gets stirred in like an additive to consciousness. These can be either wholesome or unwholesome—healthy or toxic—and can thus either clarify or contaminate the mind's ability to know itself and its environment.

The image of polluted water is elaborated upon in the Numerical Discourses.[10] "Suppose there is a bowl of water . . ." says the *sutta*, impinged upon in some way by an external factor that pollutes its depths or agitates its surface. Under such circumstances, "If a man with good sight were to examine his own facial reflection in it, he would neither know nor see it as it really is." The text goes through a list of mental states called the five hindrances, showing how each one in its own way can obscure the natural luminosity and reflective ability of the mind:

Sense desire, the subtle inclination of the mind toward alluring objects, is said to be like a bowl of water "mixed with lac, turmeric, blue, or crimson dye." The pellucid quality of the mind is spoiled by dumping such distorting and obscuring substances into its clear waters.

Ill will, the equally subtle inclination of the mind away from all disturbing or unpleasing objects, is said to be like "water being heated over a fire, bubbling and boiling." Even in English we share this sense of anger and hatred as fires that heat the mind up with destructive emotions. Boiling furiously, the mirroring capability of the mind is lost.

Sloth and torpor, those mental factors contributing to sluggishness, sleepiness, or laziness of mind, are likened to "water covered over with water plants and algae." Such growths take root in indolence and a lack of diligence, and they so encumber the mind that its surface becomes obscured.

Restlessness and remorse, their opposite qualities, are identified with "water stirred by the wind, rippling, swirling, churned into wavelets." When the mind is agitated by gales of anxieties, hyperactivity, multitasking, or incessant internal chattering, it is not capable of seeing things as they are.

Doubt is the hindrance that causes us to lack confidence, questioning ourselves, our actions, our teachers, and almost everything else. It is said to be similar to "water that is turbid, unsettled, muddy, or placed in the dark." Here too the conditions for the mind's natural reflectivity are hampered so much that it cannot function.

Such a model of the mind encourages us always to take on the dual projects of tranquilization and purification. Meditation can be understood as an enterprise of quieting the mind, so as to allow its surface to settle into a reflective plane. But the quality of the water itself also needs attention. This involves, among other things, examining its depths for the presence of toxins, neutralizing these contaminants at every opportunity, and developing diligent moral habits to ensure that new pollutants are dumped into the mind as little as possible. Fortunately the texts also offer a set of antidotes for each of these poisons, so pouring in such dispersants as nonattachment, loving kindness, energy, tranquility, and confidence is sure to have a wholesome purifying effect.

It can be exceedingly difficult to entirely shut off the source of toxic influxes into the mind, especially those that flow in from the deepest reaches of the psyche. This is only finally accomplished by an awakened one, an arahant or buddha. Yet there are plenty of ways that we can stem the flow, working each moment to calm the waters, siphon out the debris, and catch glimpses of what the world looks like when the mind is able to let it all come and go without attachment, appropriation, or interference. It can be a luminous sight.

BAIT AND SWITCH

One of the many controversies growing up around the notion of mindfulness is whether or not one can be mindful of unwholesome states, such as anger or hatred. On one hand is the view that it is possible to be mindful of anything, and it is precisely by becoming mindful of unwholesome states that one is able to abide in such states without judging them and then either suppressing them or acting them out. On the other hand there is the view that, since mindfulness is a wholesome state and anger and hatred are unwholesome states, and since one cannot experience two such opposite states in the same mind-moment, it follows that what appears to be mindfulness of unwholesome states is actually the rapid modulation between one and the other, between moments of mindfulness and moments of anger.

I would like to argue here in defense of the second position, and offer classical support for it. At the same time, however, I would like to suggest an effective method of bait-and-switch that allows us to use the classical model to neutralize unwholesome states and steer the mind stream toward the cessation of suffering. What view we take of the mechanics of liberation is ultimately less important than having the ability to employ it in our own experience to bring about transformation.

There can be little doubt that, when one looks carefully, one is not able to hold two things in mind in the very same moment (such as when driving and texting). When it appears we are doing this, we are using a kind of peripheral thought, much like peripheral vision, to hold some information in short term memory or below the threshold of conscious awareness, but when we look more closely at the experience we will find that to know one thing very clearly we need to withdraw attention from other competing data. As the Buddha puts it:

> If one frequently thinks and ponders upon thoughts of ill will, one has abandoned the thought of non–ill will and one's mind inclines to thoughts of ill will.[11]

There can also be little doubt, I think, that mindfulness is a wholesome state. It is a *sankhāra*, a volitional response or attitude toward the object of experience that is cognized by consciousness. Mindfulness is an attitude of confident equanimity, a presence of mind in which the object is neither favored nor opposed. Anger and hatred are also *sankhāras*, as are all the other unwholesome states, but these are responses characterized by aversion—a very different emotional tone than mindfulness. One simply cannot experience aversion and equanimity in the same moment, as they are vastly different qualities of mind. Yet one may be able to cycle quickly between these two states, as the mind so habitually does in many situations.

I suggest that when we say we are mindful of aversion, for example, what we really mean is that we are aware of aversion, or that we are giving our attention to the state of aversion. One of the casualties of the success of mindfulness as a trend in psychotherapy and as an object of scientific study is that it often gets confused with mere attention. According to the models of Buddhist psychology, it is possible to pay *attention* to unwholesome states of experience, and even to do so deliberately and in a disciplined manner. But attention is able to mature into *mindfulness* only in the absence of unwholesome states. When we are angry we can know very well that we are angry. But this kind of knowing is not transformative. We only become mindful of that anger when it becomes an echo or shadow of itself in a subsequent mind-moment, at which point it can be examined as a thought object with an attitude of interest and nonattachment—with mindfulness.

Here is how the bait-and-switch works, taking anger as an example: If one is furious, it will not work to simply direct someone to "Be mindful of your anger." The force of the anger is so strong, and its emotional momentum so compelling, that it is not capable of clearing out of the mind for a moment to allow true mindfulness to emerge. However one can direct a person to pay attention to bodily manifestations of the anger: "How does your body feel when you are angry?" Invited to explore these physical symptoms in greater and greater detail, an attitude of careful investigation can gradually develop. "And how does that nuanced texture of the constriction of muscles in your jaw when you are angry change in subtle ways from one moment to the next?"

By now our subject has loosened their hold on the thought or memory that provoked the anger and has been guided into some consecutive moments of mindfulness of the body. With some wholesome momentum thus established, one can gradually steer them back to investigating the emotion of anger itself. But now that anger is no longer the burning emotional charge that regards all objects of experience with ferocity, but rather it has become a thought or memory of the emotion and is thus a mind object rather than a *sankhāra*. As such it can be examined with equanimity and with mindfulness. The anger no longer holds the mind in its grip; it is regarded at arm's length, so to speak, as an object of interest.

It is only under such circumstances that mindfulness becomes transformative. One can pay attention to one's anger all day, accepting it and allowing it to manifest without judgment as it burns its way deeper into the heart. But it is not until one is able to abandon that anger, if only for a moment, that the stage becomes available to mindfulness, and it is only when mindfulness is given a chance to settle itself deeply into one's habits and character traits that the ground becomes gradually less hospitable for the cultivation of anger and more fertile for the growth of wisdom. One gradually sees, with ever-increasing clarity, that anger is just an impermanent and impersonal emotional state, fueled by a selfish and fearful self, and that it only gives rise to suffering. With such insight, unwholesome states gradually arise less often and with less intensity.

Attention needs to evolve into mindfulness, if mindfulness is to evolve into wisdom.

GROWING PAINS

There have been a lot of concerns voiced lately about the possible harmful effects of meditation practice. The pendulum is swinging back against the story that mindfulness is universally beneficial, and we are increasingly cautioned by researchers to look honestly at the cases where people suffer significant psychological stress and even trauma when engaging in rigorous meditation practice. I would like to push back a little against this push back, arguing that an important distinction is to be made between means and ends.

It is to be expected that serious psychological transformation involves some level of discomfort and difficulty. Indeed, learning how to tolerate exposure to discomfort and gaining the ability to confront and overcome difficulty has a lot to do with what makes a person grow in new ways. The knack is to know how much of this is healthy, even if painful, and at what point it may become unhealthy. The Buddha offers the analogy of a physician healing a wound—much pain is involved with its cleaning, probing, and bandaging, but such pain is necessary to the healing process. No Buddhist would want to see people suffer, however, and in situations of real psychological harm intensive meditation is clearly contraindicated.

It is useful to distinguish between mindfulness as a mental state, on one hand, and the unskillful pursuit of this state, on the other. Consider the case of a person plunging into the jungle in search of a beautiful and healing flower, who gets torn up by thorns and battered by branches in the process. The problem is not that the flower itself is harmful, only the means of pursuing it. A similar confusion exists when researchers say "mindfulness can be harmful" when what they really mean is something like "going into prolonged situations of silence and isolation, with unrealistic or uninformed expectations, under the inadequate guidance of an unsuitable teacher, when one has a history of psychological fragility, can be harmful."

Mindfulness is a *sankhāra*, a mental/emotional/behavioral state that arises and passes away in a moment in conjunction with consciousness and other functions such as feeling and perception. Coarising with such factors as trust, equanimity, nonattachment, and loving kindness, it is an inherently healthy state. Mindfulness as a mental state is always healing and never afflictive; mindfulness meditation is the practice of cultivating this benevolent quality of mind, moment after moment, and learning to sustain it even in challenging circumstances.

There are many other *sankhāras* arising in the mind that are not healthy, not helpful, and not skillful. These flavor consciousness with states such as anger, fear, hatred, cruelty, restlessness, delusion, greed, and other afflictive emotions. When this happens we are suffering, and it is exactly this kind of suffering that the entire Buddhist path is designed to heal.

Meditation alone, understood as the training of attention to focus upon a chosen object and holding it there over multiple mind-moments, whether on a fixed target as in concentration practices or a moving target with insight practices, can create the conditions for healthy *or* unhealthy mind states to occur.

The critical question becomes one of skillful means. What are the best ways to use attention training to abandon unhealthy states and cultivate healthy states? For some people, going into a retreat environment of sustained silence provides an ideally supportive setting for this. For others, these are exactly the wrong conditions, and such an environment has the opposite effect. There are even those of us for whom it starts out one way, winds up the other, or fluctuates often between being the best and worst of worlds. But when things go wrong, it is not because of mindfulness; it is rather due to the lack of mindfulness.

Here is a simple five-part model that can help clarify the course of meditation training, courtesy of the Abhidhamma:

1. Wandering Mind. The mind in its natural state is uncontrolled and free to wander. Its wanderings are never random, but follow a path shaped by bodily sensations, sensory cues, and internal habits that are largely outside our conscious awareness. Also known as the default mode, this describes our mind as we walk down the street, notice things that move or make a sound, reflexively step around obstacles, and generally daydream about the past and future.

2. Focused Mind. Here we decide to meditate and so sit down on a cushion with our backs straight, deliberately place our attention on a particular object, and try to hold it there with some steadiness. We may repeat a word internally, focus on bodily sensations as we breathe, or in some other way harness the mind and direct it consciously and intentionally. Of course it will still wander off the chosen point, but when this happens we notice it, let go of wherever we were headed, and gently return attention to the primary object (repeating as necessary).

3. Afflicted Mind. Quite often, even when the mind is successfully focused on a single object, various unpleasant and disturbing emotional states will manifest. Perhaps it is some form of restlessness, agitation, or turmoil; or a subtle or intense yearning for gratification; or annoyance at a sound, a recurring thought, or an uncomfortable bodily pain. These afflictions can be minor incidents to be explored with inter-

est and then abandoned, or they can flare up, grab hold of the mind, and rage out of control to inflict real suffering and even cause mental harm.

4. Mindful Mind. At other times when the mind is focused, an emotional attitude of mindful equanimity arises. In these cases the awareness feels soft, tranquil, trusting, and gentle, and at the same time light, agile, alert, capable, and clear. Evenly poised in the middle between attraction and aversion, it is able to regard anything under its view with profound equanimity, neither favoring nor opposing what is happening in the moment. With mindfulness thus established, the mind can begin to see things as they actually are.

5. Wise Mind. This creates the conditions in which wisdom can arise, over and above the mindfulness. One is able to observe viscerally the impermanence, unsatisfactoriness, and selflessness of all experience, and understand things in such a way that the deep unconscious patterns and structures of the psyche are transformed. The underlying tendencies toward greed, hatred, and delusion are diminished, while those toward generosity, kindness, and wisdom are strengthened.

Recognizing that a *wandering mind* can easily get entangled with suffering and cause harm to ourselves and others, we undertake the training of a *focused mind*. What we see as we look inward with growing stability and clarity is an *afflicted mind*, besieged by all sorts of unhelpful mental states. The appropriate strategy here is to notice them, understand that they are harmful, and abandon—not suppress—them. We access a *mindful mind* only occasionally and fleetingly at first, but eventually the afflictions diminish in frequency and intensity and mindfulness can become established. This allows a *wise mind* to gradually emerge and develop, leading us away from suffering and in the direction of awakening.

When in this process we get lost in the wilderness of afflictive emotions, by all means let's find skillful remedies to extricate ourselves from difficulty and get back on track. But let's also understand that the flower of mindfulness is not the cause of these difficulties, but remains their best solution.

3 Nonself

Whatever is not yours, abandon it.
What is it that is not yours?
Material form, feeling, perception,
formations, consciousness.
These are not yours.
When you have abandoned them,
that will lead to your welfare
and happiness for a long time.[12]

I THINK I AM

The Buddha may have had deep insight into the selflessness of all phenomena, but I sure do feel a lot like a self. I can see at least five ways in particular that this sense of being a self is supported.

First I feel as though I am the *occupant* of my body, the one who inhabits it. When I stand over here, I find myself at the center of the world I am constructing as various strands of sensory information are synthesized into coherent meaning. And when I walk across the room, that world-building apparatus seems to move right along with the body. I cannot help but view this body as the basis of the world I am constructing, and I feel entirely and exclusively identified with it.

Second I have a strong sense of being the *beneficiary* of the feeling tones that coarise with every moment of experience, the one who experiences both pleasure and pain. When the feeling tone is pleasant, I am the enjoyer of that pleasure; when it is painful, I am the victim of that pain, the one to whom it happens. Nobody else suffers from this toothache, and only I have direct access to the joyful contentment I feel while admiring the beauty of this sunset.

Third I am the *artiste*, the person who expresses myself. John Lennon may be right when he says "There's nothing you can sing that can't be sung," but I still feel that I am composing and enacting something special much of the time. However humble my creations, they feel like they come uniquely from me. Each of us has a creative narrator functioning within us, and as we put our hand (or pen, brush, musical instrument, etc.) to work, there is a tangible sense that we are expressing our *selves*.

Fourth I also feel like an *agent*, the one who makes choices, who acts out those choices, and who experiences the consequences of those actions. Sometimes I do good, and sometimes I do harm, but either way I have the sense of being the person who is acting in the world and at the same time being the one who is responsible for those actions. When the outcome is favorable, I deserve the praise; when it is unfortunate, I am usually (though not always) willing to take the blame. Indeed, words like decision, action, and responsibility can only make sense when there is a person who makes the choice, does the deed, and inherits the consequences.

Fifth and finally, I cannot help having the view that I am some sort of *essence*, that I somehow consist of the awareness of all the above and more. The sheer "givenness" of consciousness, the bald fact that moments of awareness rise and fall in rapid succession in this particular stream of experience, provides the basis for a continuous sense of self. I am that upon which it all depends, around which it all congeals, the very heart of all that unfolds here and now as "me."

Does all this self-making mean I am particularly dense and incapable of understanding the Buddha's doctrine of nonself? No. In fact all these assumptions are natural, and even to be expected. They are not, however, entirely as they appear.

The Buddha never said there is no self, only that the self is a mistaken interpretation of experience. When cataloguing the phenomenologically real aspects of experience discernable in meditation, the Buddha parses the apparent self into five aggregates or categories. Each of these serves as a basis for construing the self, for constructing the sense of there being *a person who* . . . , but each falls well short of actually qualifying as a self. The aggregates of material form, feeling, perception, formations, and consciousness serve as the basis for our taking on the view of being *the person who* is the occupant, the beneficiary, the artiste, the agent, and the essence, but in fact these functions are unfolding without belonging to, happening for the sake of, or in any other way constituting a self. Such a view of ourselves is very common, understandable, and even, perhaps, inevitable. But it is nevertheless merely a view.

Collectively these five assumptions add up to the mother of all views, the view of self as a really existing entity. In Pali, the word for this is *sakkāya-diṭṭhi*, and when asked how it comes to arise, the Buddha answers, quite simply, that it arises when we regard the aggregates as "this is mine, I am this, this is my self." Self, in other words, is a projection of ownership onto all experience (this is *my* body, these are *my* feelings, perceptions, formations, and this is *my* consciousness). The five aggregates really do occur—that is not in question. They just don't belong to anybody. Experience occurs, but the person who owns it is an additional construction.

If the self is so simply created, it is just as simply abandoned. In the same text,[13] the Buddha says that there is a practical way leading to the cessation of the view of self as a really existing entity: regard the aggregates as "this is not mine, I am not this, this is not my self."

Why does such an apparently minor shift in perspective make such a huge difference? It turns out that so much of the harm we do to ourselves and others is triggered by this very sense of ownership and identification. If someone were to walk off with something I felt no attachment to, I would be entirely undisturbed. But if they took from me something I cherished, something I deeply felt belonged to me, it would immediately evoke greed, hatred, and a host of related unwholesome emotions and behaviors.

The self attitude causes suffering, the nonself attitude does not. It is as straightforward as that. This is the pivotal insight of the Buddha, and it is meant to be investigated in your own (so to speak . . .) experience.

CASTLES MADE OF SAND

Perhaps you will go to the beach sometime this summer and have a chance to watch children at play in the sand. How engrossed in their projects they can get! When building a sand castle, nothing in the world seems more important than shaping it, embellishing it, and protecting it from the encroaching sea or from other children who might threaten it. This must be a timeless pursuit, for the Buddha offers the following image in a discussion with an elder monk named Radha in the Connected Discourses:

> Suppose, Radha, some little boys or girls are playing with sand castles. So long as they are not devoid of lust, desire, affection, thirst, passion, and craving for those sand castles, they cherish them, play with them, treasure them, and treat them possessively.[14]

But sand castles, then as now, are a symbol of impermanence, and will eventually slip into the sea. Equally impermanent are the affections of young children, and even before the tide comes in you may witness the gleeful demolition of what only moments earlier had been so deeply revered. Once the tide of their own attachment has turned, children can destroy what they have so carefully created with joyful abandon. This is something noticed by the Buddha as well:

> But when those little boys or girls lose their lust, desire, affection, thirst, passion, and craving for those sand castles, then

they scatter them with their hands and feet, demolish them, shatter them, and put them out of play.[15]

This is an important observation of human behavior that can of course be applied to a much wider field of understanding. It points to the remarkable insight that meaning is not something existing inherently in things but is something projected onto things by the application of human awareness. We make things important by investing them with importance, by placing our attention on them, and by treating them as valuable. Sand castles are not universally important or unimportant. When a person considers them meaningful and pays careful attention to them, they become important. When that meaning-creating enterprise is withdrawn and turned upon a different object, the sand castle becomes instantly insignificant. I have always liked the way Chuang Tzu has put it, "What makes things so? Making them so makes them so."

The Buddha appears to be using this image primarily to help Radha get unstuck regarding the concept of self. When we cling tightly to our bodies, feelings, perceptions, emotional responses, and consciousness, considering them to be profoundly important, the outcome is the sand castle of the self, attended by behaviors that contribute to greater personal and collective suffering. We construct a strong sense of self by investing the five aggregates with the view "This is me, this is mine, this is my self"; when this happens all sorts of primitive reflexes spring to life, compelling us to cling to what belong to ourselves and fight off any threat to the things we decide to own. The craving at the heart of this impulse is so fundamental the Buddha identifies it in the second noble truth as the cause of suffering. Almost all the difficulties we face, both personally and collectively, are rooted in the fact that we are choosing to define ourselves as the owners of our experience and all that flows from it.

Radha is being shown that this is just a choice that one makes and that an alternative attitude is possible. We can just as easily reverse this if we choose and regard our experience as "This is not me, this is not mine, this is not my self." If someone walks off with something that does not belong to us, or kicks a pile of sand that we have not invested with our own sense of self, then we tend to be entirely unconcerned and respond with equanimity. This does not make the aggregates disappear, any more than a child scattering her creation makes the sand cease to exist. In fact nothing in the external world has changed one bit. The difference between suffering and the end of suffering lies entirely in an internal adjustment of our attitudes.

This has wider implications as well, pointing to a second lesson of the sand castles. Much of European history's religious and philosophical endeavor discounts personal experience as unreliable and has thus focused on discovering the truth that lies behind appearances. Buddhist thought, by contrast, has been distrustful of the idea of objective truth and has been more concerned with investigating the process of experience itself. These observations have led to the insight, consistent with recent postmodern approaches to many subjects, that meaning is something created rather than discovered.

If this is correct, that value is constructed by people rather than given by nature, then the world we inhabit is a reflection of the quality of our own minds. When greed, hatred, and delusion are shaping the intentions, the actions, and the dispositions of human beings, then the world they create will reflect these attitudes. The dominant economic model might be based on controlled mutual exploitation, an excessive focus may be placed upon building and deploying systems of violent destruction, and the deliberate distortion of information could become commonplace. But if the Buddha's discovery is accurate, this does not need to be the outcome.

What if it were different than this? What if the central organizing principles of our creations were generosity, kindness, and wisdom? This is not out of the question, since we have these healthy roots in our natures alongside the unhealthy roots. We might just decide to withdraw our care from the things we have created that do such harm, and "put them out of play" as the Buddha puts it above. We might then build an economic model based on mutual generosity, develop and deploy systems of kindness and compassion, and habituate ourselves to honesty in all pursuits. Since we are all just playing in the sand anyway, why not decide to play nice?

SIMPLE AWARENESS

The human mind has a tendency to make everything it takes up more complicated and elaborate than it needs to be. You may have noticed this. The Buddhists even have a word for it, *papañca*, which means something like mental proliferation.

Meditation moves us in the other direction. It is an attempt to remove, piece by piece, layer by layer, all the baroque ornamentation with which we embellish our world of constructed experience. Underneath all the drama, the restlessness, the hopes and fears, behind the narratives we weave about ourselves, and even before we've thought of ourselves as ourselves, lies a simple, unadorned awareness. It's not even a thing—just an event that happens, a little burst of knowing, deep in the center of it all.

Experiencing this awareness has more to do with subtraction than with addition or multiplication. René Descartes was on its trail in his *Meditations* when he imagined all the complexities of our world to be an illusion. Take away everything with which we populate the story, and what is left? Just me, the thinker. The Buddha got two steps further than Descartes, beyond the "me" and beyond the thinker: instead of "I think therefore I am" we need only say "thinking occurs," or even more simply, "awareness occurs." Knowing as an event is not done by anyone, does not belong to anyone, nor need it be constrained by the thinking of thoughts.

This is an alien idea for many in the modern world. So much of our mental activity consists of thoughts, images, concepts, and words, it seems inconceivable that the mind might manifest in powerful ways devoid of thought. Yet you can feel this for yourself, here and now. It might take some practice, and twenty minutes of letting go of one thing after another, but the simple event that is consciousness, that unadorned episode of awareness, is accessible to direct experience. Like looking at the dimmest of stars in the night sky, it slips away if you try to pin it down. But if you learn to release hold of the clutter, and pry the mind out of the grooves and channels in which it is accustomed to run, you can feel it spilling out and spreading formlessly in new directions.

One of the most basic structures of the mind taught by the Buddha is that consciousness manifests in six modes, flows through six channels, or passes through six doors (choose your preferred metaphor). Consciousness is always aware *of* something, and it accesses six kinds of objects by means of six different organs. The sensory organs (eye, ear, nose, tongue, and body) and the mental organ (mind/brain) comprise an apparatus that is capable of processing information, each being sensitive to a particular type of data. The objects of experience consist of the information processed by the organs, and since there are six of them there are six kinds of things of which we can be aware (sights, sounds, smells, tastes, touches, and thoughts).

Notice that thoughts are only one of these six strands of experience. Do we spend one sixth of our time thinking about things and the rest of the time immersed in sensory experience? Hardly. We tend to operate in thinking mode almost exclusively, cycling through the other senses just briefly enough to provide information for the weaving of our conceptual narratives. Don't believe me? Try practicing mindfulness of the body.

The first step in establishing mindfulness is to switch over to channel five, the stream of tactile bodily sensations, a tactic that serves to disrupt the tyranny of the thinking organ. That the attention wanders so easily and continually off the breath and into a story line demonstrates its habitual dominance. With patient and diligent practice, however, one can train oneself to be intensively aware of bodily sensations for many mind-moments in a row. One comes to know the breath directly and intuitively, unmediated by concept, narration, or word.

The mind is now operating just as intensively as when we are thinking, but we are not thinking. We are being aware, not of the cognitive content of our thoughts, but of the universe of microsensations that are bursting within the body every moment. Or perhaps we are intently aware of the nuances in the sound of a bird's call, the rush of a passing car, or the cough of a person behind us in the meditation hall. Once just a data point to embellish our story, these sounds, when attended to without commentary, expand to become a vast territory encountered directly with awareness. The *information* provided by the senses is no longer of great interest, and it serves merely as a support for something far more captivating, the *quality* of knowing.

Awareness itself becomes the most compelling object of awareness. This simple knowing, so peaceful, so clear, so open, seems diminished by and even wasted upon the narrow confines of mere thoughts. As the thinking about things is gradually squeezed out of the mind by filling the senses with awareness, and as each experience is allowed to flow through the point of focus without obstruction, we begin to get a glimpse of a profound simplicity. Everything is changing, everything is interdependent—and there is no one to whom any of it belongs.

This awareness is nothing special. It's natural. In fact it may be the most natural, the only natural, thing there is. There is no need to magnify it by saying it is transcendent or that it permeates the quantum soup of the cosmos, or to cast it beyond time by calling it primordial or eternal. That is just the proliferation talking. If anything, it feels radically embodied, excruciatingly fragile, and entirely contingent. If a tiny microbe goes awry, or some strand of genetic material gets misread, or even if you delay the in-breath by a few too many seconds, it can all fall apart in the blink of an eye. This, too, is just another story.

Let's see if we can keep it simple. If we have to call it anything, let's call it a gift, and take joy in unwrapping it, again and again, each moment.

WAKING UP

I believe awakening is possible, in this very lifetime. This is one of the ideas we are invited to discard as modern secular Buddhists, along with belief in rebirth, heavenly beings, and miraculous powers. I prefer to suspend judgment and remain agnostic on the latter three, neither saying "If the Buddha said so, it must be so" nor "It can't be, therefore it isn't." But awakening is another story. I think it can be literally possible for a person, even a rather ordinary person, to awaken. Furthermore I think it is a goal to which we can all aspire.

Awakening (aka "enlightenment"—but this is not a good translation of *bodhi*) is understood in the early discourses as a process of gradual mental purification that culminates in a profound psychological transformation. This happened to the Buddha while seated under the Bodhi tree in Uruvela (now Bodhgaya), and something else happened to him forty-five years later while lying on his right side between two Sal trees in Kusinara. I have no idea how to understand the Buddha's *parinirvana*, his final passing away after eighty years as a human being, partly because when he was asked what happens to a *tathāgata* (buddha) beyond death, he refused to answer.

I am actually okay with his silent response and am happy to leave the matter of "what happened to him" to the Buddhist theologians who tackled it in the centuries after his last days. But getting some handle on what happened to the Buddha under that tree is more accessible, particularly since he talked about it quite a lot in language both empirical and psychological. In the earliest strata of Buddhist discourse, awakening is not about transcending this life as much as accessing the deepest levels of inherent well-being in this mind and body, here and now.

Simply put, there are emotional and behavioral habits within us, many deeply embedded, that are toxic and cause suffering. Greed, hatred, and delusion, along with the many emotions stemming from these, may sometimes be gratifying and even useful in the short term, but they invariably cause harm to oneself or others (or both). Think of chemical toxins such as caffeine, sugar, nicotine, opioids, or alcohol that can have pleasurable immediate effects but cause damage to our biological health over time. Psychological health is not unlike physical health, insofar as it can be diminished or enhanced by behaviorally adjusting the levels of poisons and nutriments in the system.

The Buddha showed us through his example that it is possible to become radically healthy and then live out one's life in this world. His awakening consisted of so transforming his mind that toxic states rooted in greed, hatred, and delusion no longer occurred, while the full range of healthy emotions and other cognitive capabilities remained active and fully engaged. Is this such an impossible act to follow? Many of his followers apparently succeeded in freeing their minds by following his instructions, leaving us in their stanzas compelling images of a person deeply at peace. Why should we not aspire to the same thing?

We know we are all capable of generous actions, compassionate words, and insightful thoughts. We also know that when we commit a selfish act, speak a hurtful word, or indulge the wishful thinking of a deluded thought, we are not entirely *compelled* to do so. We have *some* influence on what we choose to experience from moment to moment, and can, through conscious intervention, make a healthier choice even in the presence of an unhealthy impulse. Is it such a stretch to think this modest fulcrum point might be made to move the world, given a lever of sufficient length? If we can somehow manage to be kind instead of cruel in this moment, why not the next?

There are many good-hearted people in this world. There are many who are truthful and trustworthy, who do what is right more often than not, who sacrifice for the sake of others, who spontaneously feel kindness and compassion. There are some who understand everything is moving and flowing around them, and that one thrives by letting go rather than holding on. There are those at peace, who are deeply well, even in challenging circumstances. We may not be able to point to any one person and say they are perfectly awakened, their minds free forever from the three poisons, but surely we can recognize moments of awakened behavior when we see them.

Though the Buddha woke up suddenly and unshakably, I don't think we need to regard awakening in such an all-or-nothing way. Life is a series of mind-moments, each one a new creation. Every moment we inherit something from our past, transform it in our present experience, and thereby seed the consequences that will unfold in our future. Each moment the toxins we encounter may be either compounded or abandoned. A moment without greed, hatred, or delusion is an awakened moment. A person may not be considered awakened unless the toxins are thoroughly eliminated, but even an unawakened person can have an awakened moment. As the Buddha puts it:

> If one shows kindness with a clear mind—
> Even once!—for living creatures,
> By that one becomes wholesome.[16]

My suggestion is simply that as we walk the path we not look up so much at the destination, high above in the mist, but carefully place one foot in front of the other. A path keeps us centered, guiding us from veering right or left into dangerous territory. It may also deliver us to the summit, but only if each step is well taken. Every mindful moment in which generosity displaces greed, compassion takes the place of hatred, and insight dislodges delusion is a moment in which we are awake. If we can manage one moment of wisdom, why not another?

4 Understanding Ourselves

The sage understands how "all is conditioned,"
And understanding conditioning, he's free.[17]

MIND COMES FIRST

Three little words begin the *Dhammapada*, that most beloved and most translated of all Buddhist texts: *mano-pubbaṅgama dhammā*. What do these words mean? If we consult a more or less random collection of translations, we discover such a dizzying array of possibilities we might wonder that such diversity can emerge from the same three words. Is Pali really such an ambiguous language that so many combinations are somehow equally correct? Are the more recent translations an improvement upon their predecessors? Is English even equipped to render this idea? And perhaps the most intriguing question of all, what is the Buddha trying to tell us?

First we should provide some context. The opening chapter of the *Dhammapada*, a text composed entirely in verse, contains a collection of paired stanzas that are meant to be taken together. The entire couplet:

All experience is preceded by mind,
  Led by mind,
  Made by mind.

> Speak or act with a corrupted mind,
>   And suffering follows
> As the wagon wheel follows the hoof of the ox.
>
> All experience is preceded by mind,
>   Led by mind,
>   Made by mind.
> Speak or act with a peaceful mind,
>   And happiness follows
> Like a never-departing shadow.[18]

I think most readers would agree that the moral lesson here is fairly straightforward. As one writer (Narada) paraphrased the message, evil begets evil and good begets good. But the mechanism by means of which this occurs turns out to be a matter of considerable profundity and subtlety. In fact the entire Buddhist system of psychology, meditation, karma, and metaphysics is neatly summarized in the phrase *manopubbaṅgama dhammā*. It is therefore worthwhile to take some time to look closely at these words and, with an array of translations on hand, to inquire into their deepest meaning. In the meantime we will get a glimpse of some of the challenges faced by a translator, and we will be in a position to judge for ourselves whether progress is being made in the popular understanding of Buddhism.

Mano

The first word, *mano* (more correctly discussed as *manas*), is one of the three primary words for mind. The other two are *citta* and *viññāna* (*vijñāna* in its Sanskrit form). Sometimes these three terms are used interchangeably as simple synonyms, while in some cases each brings out a different aspect of mind. When delicate distinctions are being made, we might find *manas* used more precisely to refer to the means or instrument of cognition, *citta* applied to the product or content of a mind-moment, and *viññāna* reserved more for consciousness as a process or activity. Because of the common interchangeability of these three terms, we might understand how *manas* is sometimes translated as "consciousness" in the *Dhammapada* verse, but a bit more explanation is needed for its translation as "perception" and "heart".

Mind (*manas*) is an organ of mental experience, just as the eye, ear, nose, tongue, and body are organs of sensory experience. We are able to use these organs as instruments to cognize or become aware of a world of objects. While visual awareness (seeing) arises in conjunction with the eye and visual forms, and auditory awareness (hearing) arises in conjunction with the ear and sounds, and so forth, mental awareness arises in conjunction with the mind (*manas*) and mental objects (*dhammā*). We might loosely call this process "thinking," but it actually goes far beyond this to denote any mental activity not otherwise directly involving the other senses, such as imagining, remembering, planning, etc. The use of the word "perception" in translating our phrase is therefore justified insofar as the mind as a perceptual organ is needed for the construction of any mental states. It is also quite misleading, however, because Buddhist psychology has a special technical term for perception (*saññā* or *samjñā* in Sanskrit), which is not at all what the *Dhammapada* is referring to here.

The replacing of "mind" with "heart" for *manas* is also useful in bringing out the sense of volition as a key function of mind, since "heart" in English suggests a deeper seat of decision-making. But it too can have a downside, because it hints at the popular distinction of the heart as the basis of emotions while mind is relegated to rational functions only. This is a feature of Greek philosophy that has no parallel in the east. Emotions are as much mental states as anything in experience, though they are more likely to arise along with a noticeable array of physical sensations. It has become common to translate the Chinese word *shin* (Japanese *kokoro*) as heart/mind, which works well in East Asian contexts that also make little distinction between the two, but Buddhism in India encompasses a sophisticated science of mind with a technical vocabulary capable of considerable range and distinction.

The first word of the *Dhammapada* then is certainly the word for mind, but what aspect of a complex model of mind is being indicated remains to be seen from the context.

Pubbaṅgama

This compound word is made up of *pubba*, which usually means *before*, and *gama*, a form of the verb *to go* (the *n* is just thrown in there to ease the pronunciation). Mind as *going before*, as a *forerunner* or as *preceding* what follows, is generally agreed upon by our translators, but there may still be some room to debate in what sense this is to be taken. The simplest and most obvious idea is that mind *precedes in time* what follows, but here we face a major problem. In the model of the senses outlined above, both the eye and visual forms, the ear and sounds, and more importantly for us, the mind (*manas*) and mental objects (*dhammā*) are said to arise together, in the same moment of time. If this phrase is to be taken as saying that mind arises before or precedes mental states temporally, then it must be speaking about the mind in one moment preceding mental states in another moment. Alternatively, it may be using the notion of *going before* more broadly as a determining factor rather than literally as a sequence in time. Keep in mind that the ox and the cart proceed together in time, but one's path is decided by the other.

In the Middle Length Discourses there is a whole text[19] organized around the phrase "right view is the forerunner" (*sammadiṭṭhi pubbaṅgama hoti*) to the other factors of the eightfold path. As such it is a key that can be directly used to help understand any of the others. In the Numerical Discourses[20] a heedless monk is said to "lead the way" to backsliding along the path (*okkama pubbaṅgama*). In the Connected Discourses we hear that dawn is the forerunner of the rising of the sun, just as good friendship[21] and careful attention[22] foretell the arising of the seven factors of awakening. Here a useful synonym is added, where *pubbanimitta*, an "early sign," is offered alongside our phrase *pubbaṅgama* (going before).

These parallel passages suggest that in addition to priority in a sequence of time, this expression points to a guiding or conditioning influence and may be an early indicator of what will follow. When we release ourselves from the strict temporal sense of *pubbaṅgama*, it allows such broader interpretations as "mind conditions mental states" or "the quality of mind in one moment will be a leading indicator of how ensuing moments will unfold." The commentary invokes the example of a mob assailing a village. In this case asking who is foremost among the crowd refers not to who struck the first blow but to who played the leading role in inciting the attack. Such a leadership function is performed not by consciousness itself but by intention.

Dhammā

This word is among the most protean of all Buddhist terms, whether in this Pali spelling or in its Sanskrit form, *dharma*. When the final *a* is long or accented, as it is above, it is putting the word in its plural form. It therefore ceases to refer to the teaching of the Buddha and becomes a more technical word for objects of mental cognition, or for the whole realm of subjective phenomenological experience. Part of the reason it is such a shape-shifting word is that it can be used very precisely or very broadly, and it can slide up and down that continuum of meaning at will and on short notice.

In its most precise form *dhammas* are the objects that correspond with the organ of mind and the activity of mental cognition. They are the "thoughts" that "the mind" is "thinking," analogous to the "forms" that "the eye" is "seeing" or the "sounds" that "the ear" is "hearing." But these, as we saw above, coarise with one another, so it does not make much sense to say that one precedes the other in time. In its broadest sense, dhammas are all occurrences everywhere, and in later Buddhism the "realm of dharmas" (*dharmadhātu*) became a way of indicating the universe as a whole. From this perspective, the saying that "mind precedes all phenomena" could be taken as supporting forms of Buddhist idealism that hold sway in the later tradition.

In the *Dhammapada*, however, the first verse is about unwholesome states while the second verse indicates wholesome states. This helps limit the sense of the word to a middle range of all mental states that are unfolding in the experience of a particular person. Max Muller's "all that we are" is thus more apt here than Burlingame's "all things." Thanissaro's "phenomena" says it succinctly, and Fronsdal's "experience" is a useful, even elegant, innovation.

Putting it all together

The teaching encapsulated in the phrase *mano-pubbaṅgama dhammā* is first and foremost about karma. Nothing happens by chance, says the Buddha, or by divine decree or the workings of fate. According to the highly developed system of Buddhist psychology known as *abhidhamma*, every mind state (other than a few merely functional ones) is either planting causal seeds for future states or is the result of such effects from previous mind states. Almost every moment of experience, therefore, is either an ox or a cart. Or, shifting metaphors, when experiencing a resultant moment we are reaping what we have sown, and when a causative moment of experience is being constructed we are sowing what we will later reap. Understanding this interdependence between past and future, cause and effect, seed and fruit provides a powerful tool for transforming the nature of experience. It reveals both the futility of struggling against what has already arisen and the importance of skillfully influencing what is yet to come.

The means of guiding both the ox and the cart in wholesome directions is that function of the mind known as intention or will, and this is the aspect of *manas* addressed in the verse. The word for intention is *cetanā*, a variation of one of the other words for mind, *citta*, cast in a causative construction, suggesting the active function of mind that causes things to happen. Since consciousness itself merely functions to cognize or become aware of an object, it remains up to its coarising mental factors to determine what *quality of mind* is manifesting in any given moment. All such qualities are the realm of formations (*saṅkhāra*, from the same root as *karma*), the function of mind that both responds to what has arisen and determines what action of body, speech, or thought will be constructed. The Buddha saw that mental action—the churning of the mind on the meditation cushion, for example, while body and speech are outwardly tranquil—has just as much an impact on what will ensue in experience as grosser forms of action.

Our verse is saying that the quality of intention manifesting in any given moment has a direct causal influence on all that will ensue in subsequent mind-moments, which is why so much care needs to be given to how we hold ourselves each and every moment. Learning how to take care of the quality of mind in the moment is where meditation comes into the picture. Notice, in your own everyday experience, how annoyance breeds discontent, how jealousy leads to ill will, or how anger causes suffering for yourself and others. Notice also how kindness will loosen tight emotions, how generosity evokes reciprocity, and how mindfulness improves almost any situation. Seeing this for ourselves, we can gradually learn to guide our actions more skillfully in ever more wholesome directions. With wisdom at the reins rather than heedlessness, we might even entice the ox to lead our cart to freedom.

THE FIRST PERSON

The unique thing about each person's lived experience is, well, its uniqueness. Because everything is changing all the time, every single thing that happens is new. The entire universe is in a fresh configuration every moment. There may be patterns that repeat, but no two sets of phenomena are exactly the same, ever.

Human consciousness is a natural part of all this. The mind is an apparatus that creates experience, using the senses of the body and the neurons of the brain. With an alchemy we still don't have the means to understand very well, a moment of awareness arises when one of the six sense bases comes in contact with a particular stimulus, and the information is shaped into a knowable object. Each moment's experience is further accompanied with its own inimitable combination of feeling tone, interpretive perception, and emotional response, all of which occur in an instant and then cease. Consciousness is thus a series of episodic events, flashing again and again as phenomena are cognized for an exceptional instant before they vanish, never again to reappear in the same way.

This is the territory of Buddhist spirituality. It is not a matter of getting our minds around the big picture and conceptualizing the cosmos in all its grandeur, either through a traditional mythic narrative or through accessing mystical states of nonordinary reality. Nor does it involve finding and then holding close to an unmoved mover, something changeless at the heart of all the change. Rather, it is about being there to experience the extraordinary specificity of what is occurring, by meeting each new event with a fresh mind. Every moment is a unique view of a unique territory, both of which unfold in perpetual motion. Because of the continual flux of it all, holding on to anything that has happened is futile, while being open to what is happening next is crucial.

Trying to communicate with another about our own lived experience, we find ways to convey what is happening for us. Because other people have similar experiences, what we say and do can resonate with them. We seek through our dialogue to evoke in others a sense of what we undergo, and in turn we empathize with what they are expressing in order to re-create in our own experience what has happended to them. Much of the time this is successful, but because of the uniqueness of all experience, this second-person discourse—i.e., telling someone else what is happening for you—can only ever be a shadow of what is lived directly.

When more than two people interact, and especially when a large number seek to share experience, a third-person perspective is created, broader but more detached from direct experience. Language and many other forms of symbolic expression are used to create a conceptual map that encompasses the past, the future, and a world beyond the immediate. Since these maps are developed by gradual usage, there is no single objective way of conceiving the universe and our place within it. Different cultures establish different models of shared experience, and people can employ multiple schemas as they interact with different groups. The religious and scientific traditions are among the most common and widespread examples of these conceptual maps of reality.

While much is gained in scope by shifting from our individual lived experience to the larger, conceptual maps of a culture (from the first- to the third-person point of view), a valuable texture is also lost. Because of its derived nature, this third perspective is even further removed from direct experience than secondary discourse—it is an echo of a shadow, if you will. It involves thinking about objects rather than being aware of them, describing something instead of experiencing it, and conceptualizing about things rather than cognizing them directly.

Thus when we try to share an understanding of our experience, we turn to what in Buddhist psychology is called the aggregate of perception (*saññā*) rather than the aggregate of consciousness (*viññāna*). Perception involves a sort of interpretive representation or view, while consciousness is direct knowing or immediate awareness of an object. Also communication with others requires the exclusive use of only one of the six senses—mental objects or thoughts—while direct experience can encompass sights, sounds, smells, tastes, and bodily sensations. Conceptualization offers access to a wider world beyond immediate experience, but in its pursuit of commonalities it must abandon the compelling uniqueness of the moment.

Sport enthusiasts understand the value of the exceptional. Even though a game may consist of nothing more than hitting a ball or getting it into a hole or hoop or net, there are an infinite number of ways this can be done, and almost anything can happen at any time. It is the radical specificity of the moment that is so compelling. The same is true for theater, music, dance, and any other performance art. Even if one knows what to expect and has done it a hundred times, each time is unique and *this* moment is therefore immeasurably valuable.

Meditation also teaches us the value of every moment's unique experience. You have never taken in this particular lungful of air before, and you will never do so again. This particular step, with its lifting, moving, and placing phases, is absolutely special—when you choose to attend to it carefully with your awareness. We can breathe and walk without the engagement of mindful attention, in which case the activity is just another artifact of a removed, conceptualized world. The *idea* of my breathing blends into all the other ideas that populate my conceptual world, but the uniqueness of the actual *conscious experience* of my taking this breath renders it sacred.

It is the radical transience of the world that makes it both tragic and beautiful, like the cherry blossom in Japanese aesthetics. The tragedy is that nothing actually exists—it is all passing away the instant it forms. The beauty is that we have the means to be aware of this instant—a moment to know the profound poignancy of this tiny drop of reality.

Our modern world tends to look at things from the outside, enhancing the objective and diminishing the subjective. The contemplative arts of early Indian traditions place more emphasis on the subjective perspective and can help us recover and celebrate the immense value of being right here, right now. You only have one shot at this moment—don't miss it.

TEN BILLION MOMENTS

If you go to a quiet place and sit down, crossing your legs, keeping your back straight, and maybe closing your eyes, and you then pay very close attention to what is actually happening—you will notice episodes of experience arising and passing away, flowing on one after another in a rushing stream of consciousness. Welcome to the real world.

The world of human experience is made of mind-moments. Whatever else is really out there, our lived world consists of transient moments of knowing. Again and again we construct a reality using the apparatus of the five aggregates: an object is known, felt, interpreted, and responded to emotionally. Then the event is over, and the coherence that had coalesced for that instant dissolves. Another object is served up by our sense organs or mind, and another moment of seeing, hearing, smelling, tasting, touching, or thinking takes place, again with its corresponding feeling tone, perceptual interpretation, and volitional response.

While some traditional sources suggest there may be billions of mind-moments within the time of a finger snap, I suggest we regard that as hyperbole and work with a more modest number, like the four to eight mental events per second of the brain's alpha rhythm. We are capable of much faster processing (when driving a race car, for example), and there may be groggy times when it feels like we may notice one or two states per minute, at best (before our morning coffee, for example), but for simplicity's sake let's just assume there are six discrete metaevents happening in the mind per second. That is to say a huge number of neurons, organized into various networks and subsystems, all fire in a coordinated and integrated way to construct a global moment of coherent lived experience.

If there were six moments of cognition per second, there would be 360 per minute, 21,600 per hour, and assuming seven and a half hours of sleep each night, about 356,400 mind-moments in a waking day. In a life span of seventy-seven years, one person would experience about ten billion discrete episodes of experience. That's it. This is the sum total of what is actually you, your world, your life: ten billion mind-moments.

Let's take this a step further and calculate that with about seven billion people in the world today, there are a total of forty-two billion per second or two and a half trillion mind-moments per minute enacted on the planet as a whole. While the actual number does not really matter, the fact that such a number exists is astonishing. It defines and delineates the personal and the collective universe of human experience. It is called the consciousness element (*viññāna-dhātu*) in early Buddhist texts, and it comes to be called the *dharmadhātu*, the element of dharmas or mental phenomena, in later Buddhist thought.

Because the quantity of these moments are so limited (yes, the numbers are large, but they are also inexorably finite), it becomes a matter of great importance that we attend to their quality. The Buddha makes a valuable contribution to human civilization by noticing that the emotional engagement with experience that occurs every moment may be characterized as either wholesome or unwholesome, healthy or unhealthy, skillful or unskillful. Emotions rooted in greed, hatred, or delusion are harmful and result in greater suffering for oneself and others, while emotions rooted in generosity, kindness, and wisdom are beneficial and contribute to personal and collective well-being.

So it's just a matter of doing the math. If the majority of your ten billion lifetime mind-moments are unskillful and thus unhealthy, then Buddhist tradition believes you will be reborn in a less fortunate situation the next time around. The greater the positive balance of wholesome mind states, the better your life here and now and the better your rebirth will be. The details about how this happens are pretty vague, but as a general moral compass it is useful. If the totality of your 356,400 mind-moments each day are wholesome, then you are an arahant: nirvana is defined in the early texts as the complete extinguishing of the toxic emotional fires of greed, hatred, and delusion.

This also gives us a framework for working globally toward the collective awakening of the species. As an optimist about human nature I like to think most human mind-moments are healthy—there are far more good-hearted people caring for one another out there than we tend to hear about. But I accept that the pessimist—sorry, I mean realist—position, that most people's minds are filled with darkness most of the time, is a possibility. Either way, if we adopt this simple model, human flourishing is just a matter of developing and sustaining healthy mind-moments, while restraining and abandoning unhealthy mind-moments.

Unhealthy mind states tend to arise when a person is oppressed, deprived, or threatened in some way. So working to change these conditions wherever they exist will bring about more skillful behavior worldwide. Healthy mind states are encouraged by situations of safety, care, peace, and respect, so the more we can all do to provide and sustain these conditions for others, the more the project of collective well-being will be furthered. As the Buddha put it in the Connected Discourses, "Looking after oneself, one looks after others; looking after others, one looks after oneself."[23]

Sometimes a terrible act is committed by a person who is filled with anger, fear, or hatred, and many innocent people are grievously harmed. Such cases can also release a huge outpouring of compassion, goodwill, and generosity in a much larger number of people toward the victims (and even sometimes toward the perpetrator). The overall impact on the *dharmadhātu* is often beneficial, with the positive mind states far surpassing the negative. It is almost as if a cloud of mental antibodies swarms over the collective wound to heal it.

This view of the human situation combines science, Buddhism, and social activism in a simple but profound model. Consciousness can be seen as a series of brain events taking place within a natural ecosystem, but as events rather than entities they are intrinsically empty and interdependent. One can nobly aspire to the gradual purification of both the individual and the collective mind stream, by working simultaneously to ensure one's own mind is as clear and aware as possible and to help create the conditions for others to optimize their well-being.

We are all in this together, and we haven't a moment to lose.

BLINDED BY VIEWS

Once upon a time in the city of Shravasti there lived a certain king. He instructed a servant to round up in one place a gathering of men who had been blind since birth. "The blind men have been assembled, your majesty," said the man. The king further instructed him to introduce an elephant to this group of men, such that each could examine it for himself. "This, sir, is an elephant," the servant said to each of the blind men in turn. But to the first he presented the head of the elephant, to the second, the ear, and so in turn to the rest of the blind men he presented the tusk, trunk, body, foot, backside, tail, and tuft of the tail. At this point the king approached the blind men and asked of each, "Tell me, sir, what is an elephant like?" Each answered according to his own experience, saying in turn that the elephant was like a water pot, a winnowing basket, a plowshare, a plow pole, a granary, a pillar, a mortar, a pestle, and a broom.

This much of the story is generally well known. But how it ends, and the point the Buddha was making by telling this story, is less commonly recognized. We understand the point that any single thing might have multiple different components and can be viewed from many perspectives, and that our understanding of any particular issue is going to be limited by the extent of our own direct experience. But in its original telling the story goes on to say that these nine blind men began quarrelling about the nature of the elephant, each one saying "The elephant is like this, not like that," and "The elephant is not like that, it is like this." Eventually they came to blows and began striking one another with their fists. The king who had called them all together sat back and watched, we are told, with great amusement. The entire enterprise had been set up, from the start, as an entertainment for the king.

This story is told by the Buddha in the *Udāna*[24] in response to a situation where there were many teachers of different traditions living in the same vicinity. Not only did they all have differing views, opinions, and beliefs, but they depended upon these differing views for their livelihood. And it may not entirely surprise us to hear that "they lived arguing, quarreling, and disputing, stabbing each other with verbal daggers, saying 'The Dhamma is like this, it's not like that,' and 'The Dhamma is not like that, it's like this.'" Does any of this sound familiar?

What the king seemed to know is the extent to which views, beliefs, and opinions in human beings link directly to very primitive instincts for defending what belongs to oneself and attacking what is regarded as belonging to others. The entire enterprise of creating *belonging* as part of our construction of reality, along with the sense of self to which it all belongs, is perceived by the Buddha to be the root cause of the suffering we inflict upon ourselves and others. It is one thing to have a difference of opinion with someone else; it is something else entirely to have this difference become the basis for stoking the fires of greed, hatred, and delusion.

It is entirely natural, since most issues are complex, that people will have different perspectives on them. It is also inevitable that most perspectives will derive from a limited range of experience and are unlikely to embrace the whole picture. It may be further understandable that people will express their differences of opinion, engaging in mutual dialogue and debate. What is utterly unnecessary, the Buddha seems to be saying here, is that such differences need escalate to stabbing each other with verbal daggers, striking one another with fists, and worse. At that tipping point, something profoundly unhealthy happens, as primordial mechanisms of aggression and defense kick in. Once this happens the original content of the dispute is lost and the impulses of the self take over: the need to establish oneself, defend oneself, aggrandize oneself, and generally attack and injure anything viewed as not in agreement with and thereby threatening oneself.

The problem, as usual, is not with the content but with the process. So the solution is to be found not in what we believe but in how we hold those beliefs. The solution to differing views is not some objective standard by means of which those with wrong views can simply learn what is true and change to right views. Such a reference point does not in fact exist in our postmodern world of plurality and the local construction of meaning. Rather the key to harmony is learning to differ in opinions without engaging the fatal move of saying "Only this is true; everything else is wrong."

In the *Canki Sutta*[25] the Buddha outlines some of the ways we gain knowledge: accepting it on faith; going along with what people generally approve; receiving a tradition that has been handed down through generations; working things out through reasoned argument; or accepting a view after careful reflection. He then goes on to say about each of these that regardless of what one believes, it may turn out to be "factual, true, and unmistaken" or it may turn out to be "empty, hollow, and false." Since one can seldom ever really be sure which is the case, truth is best served by recognizing a viewpoint as only a viewpoint, and refraining from taking that extra step of regarding it as true to the exclusion of all other views. In other words, all views are best held gently, rather than grasped firmly.

The point of the story is not just that most things have multiple different perspectives, but the absurdity of being attached to only one viewpoint and the harm that can ensue when one does so.

So by all means let's disagree on things, and even, if need be, let's do so vociferously. But let's also try not to take it all personally. That's when the fists start flying.

5   The Interdependence of Experience

From the unseen, states come and go,
glimpsed only as they're passing by.
Like lightning flashing in the sky
—they arise and then pass away.[26]

PINCH YOURSELF

Pinch yourself. Go ahead and give yourself a good hard pinch on the arm or the back of the hand. Now, according to Buddhist psychology, you should be able to distinguish at least three different components to the experience: the touch, the pain of the touch, and the aversion to the pain of the touch. Our mind is very good at merging these all together, but what is actually going on are three different processes, synthesized by three different brain systems, that are then synchronized with one another and interpreted as a unified experience. The *Discourse on the Establishment of Mindfulness*[27] trains us how to see this for ourselves.

The first foundation upon which mindfulness is established, mindfulness of the body, directs us to notice in great detail all our bodily sensations. Consciousness arises in six different modes (seeing, hearing, smelling, tasting, touching, and thinking) that correspond to the six sense organs of our bodies and the six kinds of objects to which each is sensitive. Mindfulness of the body is like tuning in a radio station: we are instructed to tune in only to channel five and regard the other

sense inputs as distractions. If, while noticing all the nuanced sensations of the breath, for example, one hears a sound or thinks a thought,
we are invited to gently but firmly let it go and return attention to the
"touches" of physical sensations alone. (You all know the drill.) A gentle pinch of the arm is registered as one such touch, a mere episode of
discernible physical sensation.

Mindfulness of feeling is the second foundation upon which mindfulness is established, and here we shift attention to the feeling tone
that accompanies every moment's experience. Feeling tone is measured
on a sliding scale between strong pleasure and strong pain, with sub-
tler hedonic shades in between and a neutral feeling tone at the center
point of the scale. A feeling tone arises every moment, in all six sensory
modes, and is not limited to physical sensations. Some smells are pleasant, others are so horrible it is painful to smell them. Some thoughts feel
good to think, such as pleasant memories or hopeful fantasies, while
others are so unpleasant we try hard to avoid or suppress them. A gentle
pinch on the arm can feel neutral or even pleasant, but if you pinch
hard enough you will surely experience pain. The challenge here, and it
is a considerable one, is to distinguish between the touch and its corresponding feeling tone. Can you feel the pain as something over and
above the touch? The touch is there, and then as you gradually pinch
harder you can feel the pain jump out of it, almost as if it were something else entirely—which it is.

The third and fourth foundations of mindfulness redirect awareness
again, this time to our emotional life. Awareness of an object is always
influenced by some sort of attitude or emotional response, and we learn
to pay careful attention to these. The third foundation, mindfulness
of mind, points to the general fact that when you are experiencing the
intense pain of the pinch, an emotional response of aversion is evoked
(we hate that it feels bad), while before and after this event there is no
aversion. The aversion is also a mere episode, arising and passing away
interdependently with the pain of the experience. The fourth foundation, mindfulness of mental states, explores this phenomenon in greater

detail. We can explore the pinch directly as the second of the five hindrances, by using the five-aggregate or the six sense-sphere-schemas, or as a direct experiential manifestation of the four noble truths.

We can hardly help but object to the pain of the pinch. The touch and the pain are registering information, and we are reacting to this information in a visceral and immediate way. We don't like it, we don't want it, and we experience an intense desire for the pain to go away. Unlike a machine we *engage* with our experience at all times, we *respond* to what is happening in a wide range of both innate and culturally learned ways. One of these ways is to take it personally. If someone else pinches us, we feel anger and resentment toward them, and if we pinch ourselves, we may chastise or feel sorry for ourselves. Whatever can be blamed for the discomfort (like the guy who told us to pinch ourselves in the first place!) is an easy target for our hatred.

Here is where all the trouble occurs, according to the Buddha. All six sense objects and all three feeling tones are a natural part of experience, and we depend upon these to navigate our world. Even the Buddha experienced these normally after his awakening. But how we respond emotionally to these sensations is another matter entirely, and it is in this arena that the aspiration to be a better person is played out. Some responses are primitive, unhealthy, and toxic, causing great harm to oneself and others and obstructing moral development, while others have the opposite effect.

The Buddha demonstrated how it is possible for a human being to experience the full range of sense objects and feeling tones, but to respond only with benevolent rather than with harmful emotions. Can we feel pain without getting angry, violent, or hateful? Can we feel pleasure without getting attached, enchanted, or addicted? To do so is to live as a noble human being, as one who feels deeply the joy (mental pleasure) of another's well-being or the poignant sorrow (mental pain) of the loss of a loved one, but with an attitude of calm equanimity rather than tumultuous and self-inflated emotional reactivity.

By extinguishing the fires of greed, hatred, and delusion, we are transposing our emotional range. Emotions such as kindness, generosity, compassion, confidence, and gladness for the good fortune of others continue to function, and are even enhanced by being uncovered, while the afflicted emotions that cause so much harm in our lives and our world are allowed to atrophy. When a pinch on the arm becomes an experience to be explored and unpacked with growing interest and understanding, rather than a reflexive call to arms, we are well on the way to healing all that is flawed in ourselves and the world we create. Perhaps this lesson can be extended to a collective level, where even heinous crimes can be an invitation to investigate and heal rather than to lash out and punish.

A PERFECT STORM

Why do we get angry? What, exactly, happens when we act with greed, with hatred, or with delusion? If we understood the mechanisms involved with constructing and perpetuating these toxic behaviors, it would help a lot with our ability to avoid, abandon, or transform them, and it would contribute greatly to our learning to be generous, kind, and wise instead. The matter is explained quite succinctly in the *Abhidharma-samuccaya*,[28] a Sanskrit text attributed to the Yogacāra teacher Asanga.

Three conditions need to coarise in the same moment for an unwholesome event, a *kilesa*, to occur in the mind. The first is the presence of underlying tendencies, dormant dispositions toward an unwholesome response, such as greed, hatred, and delusion. Each of us consists of a bundle of dispositions or habits, some of which are basic instincts inherited genetically from our ancestors, some of which have been laid down in early childhood, and some of which are taken up and modified each and every moment as we respond to the world. As choices are made and actions are performed, the residue or consequences of these are accumulated as latent tendencies. Modern psychologists might consider these residing in the unconscious mind, and would identify them with terms such as character or personality traits, habits, learned behaviors, conditioned responses, and the like. They build up naturally as a consequence of experience and provide a record of that experience, almost like sedimentary rocks retain information from eras long past.

One of the reasons a person gets angry is because they have a disposition toward anger. This disposition may originate as a common possession of all humans, but in each individual, depending on the particular circumstances of their life, it has become strengthened or weakened by practice. Some people are thus more disposed to anger than others, not because of fate or chance, but because they have regularly called forth and reinforced the underlying tendency toward anger by often becoming angry.

The second condition for the arising of a toxic behavior is the appearance of an object conducive to the evoking of a toxin. Every moment of consciousness will manifest as consciousness of a particular object, which may be a sight, sound, smell, taste, touch, or thought. In the case of anger, this might be hearing a sound that is interpreted as an insult, for example, or even just thinking such a thought. The object's ability to provoke anger is not an intrinsic quality of the object itself but a matter of how it is construed by the subject seeing, hearing, or thinking it. Almost anything can act as an object conducive to anger, especially for someone who has a strong disposition toward anger.

An episode of anger is thus an interaction between these two factors: a proclivity toward anger on one hand and the arising of a triggering input on the other. If either one of these conditions is not present, the anger will not occur. A calm and forgiving person, for example, without a strong disposition toward anger, might tolerate an insulting remark without getting angry, while the anger of even a habitually angry person will lie dormant until it is provoked by a particular incident. In extreme cases in either direction, some people will almost never get angry, while others seem to be continually angry.

There is a third condition for the manifestation of a toxin, namely the presence of unwise or careless attention. This has to do with the quality of the mind in the present moment, with how much attention is brought to bear upon the awareness of the object. If attention is weak or lacking, then there is little or no conscious awareness and one is acting automatically or reflexively. The toxin surges from latency and is acted out in behavior without even being noticed by the mind. You may have experienced this once or twice, becoming angry without being aware of consciously choosing to do so.

In moments when attention is strong we notice what is going on, and are thereby more able to influence what unfolds by the exercise of volition. At such times we are deliberately cultivating awareness of inner states as they arise and pass away with what the Buddhists call wise attention or careful attention (*yoniso manasikāra*). This wonderful phrase is derived from the word for womb (*yoni*) and for *making in* or *making with the mind* (*manasi-kāra*). The image of a womb evokes such qualities as protecting, nurturing, and caring, and suggests that we can incubate each state of mind with a particular quality before giving birth to a behavioral response.

It is not about denying or suppressing the emotion but about treating it with care. We may still get angry, but the experience is different when we are consciously aware that we are angry compared to when we are not. Refining the attention further, by bringing mindfulness to bear, renders the anger an object of investigation, to be regarded with curiosity and patience, rather than an emotion that has seized control of the mind and is carrying it off.

All three of these conditions—the underlying tendencies present in the mind, the objects of experience that can set these off, and the lack of skillful attention—can come together in a perfect storm to bring about an unwholesome moment, wreaking havoc on the quality of our inner lives and blustering outward to the detriment of the world as a whole. The Buddhist tradition is offering a threefold approach to reducing their strength, and possibly even calming them once and for all:

1. The practice of integrity (*sīla*) works to restrain or prevent triggering objects from arising in experience through the modulation of behavior. If we are trying to manage our anger, for example, it might be good to steer clear of the company of others who are easily angered or who habitually annoy us in order to avoid situations likely to provoke our own anger.

2. The practice of concentration (*samādhi*) trains the mind's capacity for being present in the moment, thus augmenting our ability to bring wise attention to bear as much as possible. When the powers of the mind are focused one can better see anger as it arises internally, and with such heightened awareness one can more easily remain calm even in the presence of strong provocation.

3. The practice of wisdom (*paññā*) has to do with gradually diminishing the underlying tendencies themselves in the unconscious mind. There is no need either for an act of will to restrain anger, or for behavioral changes to avoid its provocation, if the latent disposition toward anger is itself eradicated. It may be that some deeply seated habits never entirely go away, as with the urge to drink in some alcoholics, but many of the inclinations we might have felt strongly at one stage of life can entirely wither away at another. Wisdom involves such deep transformation, and as it develops the toxic states come up less often, with less intensity, and for shorter periods of time.

The Buddha has demonstrated that greed, hatred, and delusion can be eliminated entirely from human experience. Understanding the conditions that conspire to feed these tempests goes a long way in helping us calm their raging forces whenever possible.

THE BUDDHA'S SMILE

The most difficult Buddhist idea to explain, I find, is not interdependent arising or nonself, challenging as these are, but equanimity. How is it that one can neither like nor dislike something without being emotionally detached or indifferent? Our sense of identity is so bound up with our desires that to many people the thought of being without preferences for one thing or another is tantamount to being stripped of the very quality that makes us human. Nonattachment is just so *dry*. Give me the pot-bellied laughing Buddha any day (who of course is not a Buddha at all but a Chinese folk deity) over the austere figure presiding over our meditation halls with just the hint of a smile on his face.

The Buddha is not asking us to have no emotion but only to let go of our more primitive and unhealthy emotions. Desire, in both its positive mode as greed or attachment and its negative mode as hatred or aversion, is an unhealthy emotion and causes suffering. We don't see this, but it's true. We don't want this to be the case, but it is. It is easy to see at the extreme ends of the spectrum, where craving manifests as an uncontrollable addiction or hatred results in a frenzy of brutal ethnic cleansing. But even at the near end of the spectrum these same emotional forces are at work gently pulling us toward the things we want and pushing us away from what we don't want. And though the effects of this are more subtle, the heart of the Buddha's insight was to recognize that they can be just as harmful.

What is the harm, you ask, if you like the color purple or if you are mildly annoyed by people who are rude, just to take a couple of random examples? Nothing much. The problem is that desire is a house builder, as the Buddha discovered on the night of his awakening:

> Housebuilder, you have been seen! You will not build another house . . . my mind has reached the destruction of craving.[29]

It constructs the scaffolding of self, upon which suffering is then draped. Only a self has desire (unlike rocks and trees), not because it is some spiritual essence unique in nature, but because the liking or not liking of something is itself what creates the self, the *person who* likes or does not like what is happening this moment. This then creates the conditions for suffering to arise, for only a self can suffer (rocks and trees do not). We can only be disappointed if we set ourselves apart from what is happening by wanting it to be other than it is.

The crux of the second noble truth is not *what* you want, but the very fact *that* you want. Greed and hatred, even in their modest forms of wanting and not wanting, delimit and thereby restrict the mind. They carve our minds into boxes and compartments, hemming us in with habits, wishes, wants, and needs. Consciousness, which like a luminous mirror is capable of reflecting whatever object it encounters selflessly (and thus naturally), is restricted, distorted, and even perverted by the likes and dislikes of our emotional habits—even those that seem innocuous. Under such circumstances, it is impossible to see things as they really are.

The truth is we like our preferences and prejudices, we like defining ourselves in terms of what we like and don't like. It is precisely desire's entanglement with the sense of self that makes this all so difficult to unravel. Fortunately there is a relatively easy and accessible way to counter the powerful forces of desire: the cultivation of equanimity. Every moment of mindfulness is also a moment of equanimity. It is not a disengagement from the object of awareness, but rather the full and complete engagement with it. It is engaging with the breath, or with a feeling tone, or with a thought, without also either wanting it to stay as it is or wanting it to be different than it is.

Awareness without wanting is not the same as having no emotion, for equanimity itself is an emotion. If a neutral feeling tone lies at the midpoint between pleasure and pain, equanimity as an emotional response lies midway between liking and not liking, wanting and not wanting, greed and hatred. In the case of a neutral feeling tone there is still a feeling tone, just not one that is obviously pleasant or painful. So too with equanimity, there may be a powerful emotional charge, but it is not one that falls to one side of desire or the other. It may strike many of us as surprising, and even entirely alien, but the Buddhists are pointing to an intensity of emotional response that accepts and even celebrates what is happening without trying to distort it into something else, into something that *I* prefer.

Loving kindness is a good example. We care deeply for the well-being of another, but without the personal complications that come with liking or wanting them. This is not romantic love, nor even parental love, but rather a selfless love. Yes, love can reach great heights of passion when we simultaneously want someone as a lover or take pride in them as a parent, but to the extent a sense of self is implicated the emotion tips from selfless to self-referential. This does not make it wrong, only prone to generate suffering. Loving with equanimity can also be felt intensively, as can compassion, happiness, sorrow, and a host of other nontoxic emotions, without being self-involved.

We do not become less human by purging toxins from our emotional life, but more nobly human. Abandoning greed, hatred, and delusion at every opportunity, we are still left with a rich, nuanced, and more healthy emotional life. Like all other aspects of the deep and profound Dharma, this is better understood through practice than by theorizing. Explore the cultivation of equanimity in your own experience, and see if you can discover what the Buddha is smiling about.

MUSIC OF THE MIND

The story is told of a king who hears a sound he has never heard before and finds that sound to be "tantalizing, lovely, intoxicating, entrancing, and enthralling." He asks about it and is told it is the sound of a lute. He then asks that this lute be brought to him so he can see what sort of thing it is. The lute is delivered to the king, who examines it with great interest. He takes the lute apart, piece by piece, until it is little more than a pile of splinters. He then declares disdainfully, "What a poor thing is this so-called lute." Casting it aside, he asks, "Never mind this lute, bring me just the sound."

The king is patiently told, "This lute, sire, consists of numerous components, and it gives off a sound when it is played upon with its numerous components; that is, in dependence on the parchment sounding board, the belly, the arm, the head, the strings, the plectrum, and the appropriate effort of the musician."[30]

I find that this story provides a useful perspective on the modern study of consciousness. It is a widespread assumption of scientific materialism that something like the mind—the lovely sound—can be reduced to the thing that produces it—the lute—and that the proper work of understanding the mind mostly involves a closer and closer investigation of the brain. Yes, the components of the lute are necessary conditions for the sound to be produced, but the sound itself is something wholly different from the lute. Too much emphasis on the physical basis misses the point that the music of lived experience is something enacted upon the brain rather than embedded in it.

The opposite assumption is equally prevalent, that there must be something unconditioned, some essence beyond the normal matrix of cause and effect, in order to account for the sound of the lute or the experience of the mind. If consciousness is not reducible to materiality, the argument goes, it must be fundamentally irreducible, and thus either a transcendent creation or somehow part of the primordial fabric of the cosmos.

I understand this story to be pointing toward a middle way between these two positions, that the sound is an entirely natural phenomenon, but one that is implemented rather than constituted. The mind is an event that occurs, in other words, an interdependent confluence of factors that never actually exists but that repeatedly and reliably unfolds. The neurons of the brain are indeed the stage upon which our human drama is enacted, but it is the activity of their firing, changing by the millisecond, that brings our story to life. And that activity is only accessed by attending directly to lived experience.

The matter is further remarked upon by Buddhaghosa in the *Path of Purification*, where he too takes up the example of a lute to illustrate the nonmateriality of the mind. "There is no heap or store of unarisen [mind] prior to its arising. When it arises, it does not come from any heap or store, and when it ceases it does not go in any direction. There is no heap or store acting as a depository of what has ceased."[31]

In the same way the sound of a lute does not exist anywhere before or after its enactment, the sound does not come from anywhere or go anywhere. The plucking of a string is an event, requiring the lute, the string, the pick, and the effort of an efficient cause (in this case a musician). In Buddhist language both the mind and the sound of the lute "not having been, are brought into being, and having been, they vanish."

The neuron is something that stands at the intersection of space and time, much like the string of a lute. As a physical object (a living cell) it is of course extended spatially. The fact that there are so many neurons in a brain, and that each is connected to so many others in a web of such daunting complexity, invites the compelling project of mapping out its master wiring diagram. But the essence of a neuron is its function, the fact that it "fires" from time to time and that these action potentials interact with one another as they cascade through the architecture of the brain—much like what happens when a string is plucked.

From the perspective of lived experience, *where* things are happening in the head is irrelevant, while *when* they are happening is of great importance. We experience the flow of events, not the interconnection of structures. The practice of meditation involves listening closely to the music of the mind. We are not concerned in the moment about *how* things get to be the way they are, only *that* they are so very much exactly what they are. When a musician loses herself in the music, the instrument falls away—much like Dogen's "casting off the body and mind."

What consequences does this have for the way we live our lives? Notice that the story begins with the king's sense of wonder around the beauty of the sound he hears. In those five adjectives we can find all the allure of the human condition: tantalizing, lovely, intoxicating, entrancing, enthralling. Yet he ends up with a pile of splinters, missing and dismissing the very thing that first caught his attention.

By all means let's study the brain, but the conceptual model of how it works to which we aspire, fascinating though it is, pales beside what is accessible when we cast aside scrutiny of the instrument and take up instead the playing of its music. What is the experience of the sound when we pluck this string? And this next note, is it discordant or does it beautifully compliment the first? How deeply can we feel the harmony of several strings, spaced a third or a fifth interval from one another, plucked simultaneously as they resonate together?

Accounting for experience is a compelling project, but living it is far more so. Just sit quietly, and listen to the music.

6 Healing or Harming?

Are you delighted, wanderer?
  What is it, friend, that I have gained?

Are you grieving, then, wanderer?
  What is it, friend, that I have lost?

Is it, then, wanderer, that you're
neither delighted nor grieving?
  Friend—it is just so.[32]

PLEASURE AND PAIN

Many teachers have said that one of the most difficult Buddhist words to translate is *dukkha*, and I would add that *sukha* is equally challenging. Basically *sukha* just means feeling good, while *dukkha* means feeling bad, but the challenge is that we can and do mean this in so many different ways. When referring to physical experience these words usually mean pleasure and pain; in regard to mental experience, they come closer to gladness and sorrow; when applied to emotional experience, they can mean happiness and unhappiness, or extend to something like well-being and anguish. Buddhist teachings take these terms even farther to an existential level, where *dukkha* is the pervasive suffering of the first noble truth and *sukha* refers to its cessation in the ultimate welfare of awakening in this lifetime.

I suggest that what we have here is a hierarchy of nesting *sukhas* and *dukkhas*, with each higher level being capable of holding and reconciling the levels below. For example, we hear that the Buddha experienced wracking bodily pains in the final days of his life, but presumably these did not give rise to unhappiness or diminish his awakening in any way. Compare here the popular saying that while pain is inevitable, suffering is optional. In the simile of the two arrows,[33] we are told that weeping and wailing upon being struck with one arrow is like stabbing ourselves with a second arrow, the first being a physical feeling and the second a mental feeling. We also know from our own experience that stringing together moments of physical pleasure does not assure us mental happiness. In fact it is often true that physical pleasure is a direct cause of mental unhappiness—as in the case of addiction.

The physical pleasure and pain on the first rung of this *sukha/dukkha* ladder is hard-wired into the human mind and body, and is both a natural and useful aspect of human experience. The goal of practice is not to pursue pleasure and avoid pain, but rather to experience both with full awareness, neither favoring one nor opposing the other. It is thus possible to experience mental pleasure or happiness while experiencing a certain amount of physical discomfort. A beautiful day hiking in the forest need not be entirely ruined by a blister on one's foot, even though it makes itself known with every step. In the mental context of the second rung, the Pali prefixes *su-* and *du-* (meaning more or less "good" and "bad") are retained, but they are affixed to the word for mind (*manas*) to yield *somanassa* and *domanassa*, which might be translated as something like glad-minded and sad-minded.

As we ascend this ladder of evolving meaning, we recognize that much of what Buddhist teachings address is a deeper emotional *sukha* and *dukkha*, which has more to do with the aggregate of volitional formations (*saṅkhāra*) than with the aggregate of feeling. Here the sense of the words shift slightly away from pleasure and pain in the direction of health and well-being on one hand, contrasted with emotional dis-ease or distress on the other. In this context we encounter words like welfare (*hita*) and benefit (*attha*), along with their opposite forms. The Buddha taught for the welfare and benefit of all beings, and those teachings instruct us how to turn away from what is harmful to ourselves and others and cultivate what inclines to the welfare and benefit of both. We not only want to feel good and be happy, we also want to be well in a profound sense of the word. The phrases supporting *mettā* practice come to mind in this regard: "May you be safe; May you be well; May you be free from harm."

Here again I think emotional *sukha* can encompass and absorb mental *dukkha*. I would like to think that one can feel the poignant sorrow of the loss of a loved one, for example, which would be an expression of mental pain, while at the same time feeling emotionally whole and well. When an arahant calls to mind or witnesses the *dukkha* of other beings, she feels mental pain as her heart trembles in the face of suffering, yet this is held in the embrace of a deeper wellness. The two terms are no longer polar opposites; they simply function at different levels of scale.

Buddhist thought also links the notion of welfare to the ethical quality of mental and emotional states, behaviors, and traits. Ethical value is not something tacked on to things by human invention; it is built into the very fabric of consciousness. Here *sukha* and *dukkha* become entwined with the words *kusala* and *akusala* that refer at the same time to what is healthy and unhealthy and to what is skillful and unskillful. What this means is that true well-being can only come from expressions of generosity, kindness, and wisdom, while greed, hatred, and delusion will always involve some level of distress. Furthermore, welfare is a skill that can be learned by anyone, and much of Buddhist practice is indeed the practicing of this skill.

Ultimately, however, the Buddha was addressing an even higher, more far-reaching sense of *sukha* and *dukkha*, one which we might call existential. The noble truth of suffering means that even though there is gratification in sense pleasures, even though there may be moments of mental joy, and even though one might manage to be more or less healthy emotionally, there is still a deep unsatisfactoriness inherent in the human condition. No matter how blessed our lives, we all face illness, aging, and death. And no matter how much goodness we might find in this world, the entire enterprise of life is caught up with the cruelties of beings devouring one another to survive.

The solution to this deep *dukkha* is an even deeper *sukha*. Awakening is called the highest pleasure (*paramam sukham*), yet we are miles from the mere pleasure with which we started, and the word is hardly adequate to express this paramount condition of ultimate well-being. It is not freedom *from* the conditions in which we find ourselves (no eternal bliss in this tradition), but it is freedom *within* them. Even though there is physical pain, we are capable of joy; even though there is mental sorrow, we are able to be emotionally well; and even though we are part of an impermanent, selfless flow of phenomena, we are nevertheless able to feel whole, complete, and deeply healthy, and we can celebrate with our awareness all that passes before our eyes even as it slips through our fingers and vanishes forever.

DEEPER HEALTH

Research over the past decades has shown pretty convincingly that physical health is influenced by the quality of the nutrients we ingest, the activities we engage in, and the habits that guide our behaviors. Such quality is measured on a sliding scale between healthy and unhealthy. If we eat unhealthy foods, engage in unhealthy behaviors, and develop unhealthy habits, then the outcome will be further unhealthiness. The reverse is equally true, when healthy modes of living replace unhealthy ones. This is a matter of understanding the biological laws of nature and has nothing to do with moral judgment or religious decree.

More recent research is demonstrating the extent to which this principle extends also into the realm of mental health. When we are motivated by healthy intentions, engage in healthy thinking, and develop healthy belief systems, we tend to be healthier and happier. Aversion, for example, is for the most part an unhealthy emotion. While it might be effective to bring about certain changes in the short term, it also has a tendency to cause damage to ourselves and to others over the long run. A person who is chronically annoyed, or who repeatedly ruminates on hateful thoughts, is not likely to experience much well-being. And if being displeased much of the time and regularly finding fault in any situation becomes a character trait, such a person is unlikely to maintain healthy relationships. The same might be said for fear, anxiety, self-pity, obsession, compulsion, addictive patterns of behavior, and a host of other emotional states associated with mental unhealthiness.

Here, too, I think we are facing a fundamental understanding of how the natural world operates, a psychological law of nature, if you will. It is not particularly helpful to try to assign blame for these difficulties, or to couch the matter in the religious language of divine retribution. Just as realizing that "what goes up must come down" is simply a matter of understanding how the physical world works, so also there might be similar descriptive laws of psychological functioning. These might include such things as "when you are motivated by unhealthy desires, you will experience unhealthy outcomes," or "when you regularly think in healthy ways, healthy habits of mind become reinforced," or "when you activate unhealthy mental states, healthy states do not simultaneously function, and vice versa."

The Buddha said just such things about how the mind works and seemed to speak of health and well-being as a natural process of growth in understanding. In the first verses of the *Dhammapada*, for example, we find "If one speaks or acts with an afflicted mind, then suffering follows, like the cart follows the horse." And "If one speaks or acts with a clear mind, then happiness follows, like a constant shadow." In another discourse we hear "Whatever a person frequently thinks upon and ponders upon, that will become the inclination of their mind." And "If one thinks and ponders upon unhealthy thoughts, one has abandoned healthy thoughts and the mind inclines to unhealthy thoughts."[34]

Mental health in early Buddhist teachings is simply a matter of becoming acquainted with the way the mind naturally works, and then using that knowledge to gradually guide the mind away from unhealthy intentions, thoughts, and habits toward more healthy ones. Well-being is a skill that can be acquired by anyone, because it has to do with aligning oneself with the way things naturally are.

Now here is an intriguing thought: Might it be the case that what is clearly evident about physical and mental health is also true for moral health? What if morality is something built into the fabric of the natural world, rather than something tacked on by human speculation? For the most part modern thought has characterized the material world as following impersonal laws of nature, while regarding morality and human behavior as something very different. Morality has to do with the free choosing of a personal agent that is not itself embedded in the same matrix of cause and effect as the rest of nature. The body is natural, but the soul is supernatural. Hence science is a matter of understanding how the world works, but ethics is a matter of individual religious sensitivity and commitment. Such a separation can result in powerful technologies being wielded by people of underdeveloped moral sensibility.

In Buddhist thought, however, human behavior is just as much a part of the natural world as the human body and mind. And just as the concept of health can be understood in physical and mental ways, so also it can be understood morally. Such a sense of moral health is fundamentally built into the Buddhist notion of well-being. The concepts of good and bad, loosely translating the words *kusala* and *akusala*, are not defined as ideals or absolutes but in terms of their consequences for oneself and others. When you eat this, does your body become more or less healthy? When you think like that, is your mind thereby more or less healthy? And when you act in such a way, are you contributing to more or less well-being for yourself and others? All three are related by the same, deeper understanding of health that rests ultimately upon an understanding of the natural patterns of cause and effect.

That morality is a natural feature of the natural world is an insight we all have to learn if we hope to be deeply well. The more the sense of an autonomous self is injected into any situation, the more it acts as a lightning rod for the greed, hatred, and delusion that inevitably bring suffering. The more we can get the self out of the way, the more clearly we can see the effect of our thoughts, words, and actions upon ourselves and others. When behavior is purified of these toxins and is guided by an understanding of just how deeply into nature the idea of health penetrates, it is natural that we will do what is right. Research into your own experience will bear this out.

TURNING THE CORNER

It is time for us to evolve. We know well enough that species adapting to a changing environment survive, while those that do not become extinct. We also know our environment is changing, and that our own activities are contributing to those changes. We should therefore know enough to understand: we must either evolve or perish.

For the first time in history, our challenge is not the implacable forces of external nature but the inner toxins of our own nature. The radical changes in the ecosystem threatening our survival are not being thrust upon us from the outside but stem from the greed, hatred, and delusion lodged deep in our own hearts. We are our own greatest threat, and we are thus in the unique position of having to adapt both to ourselves and from ourselves.

The operating system we are using to function in this world is a relic from a previous age and is rapidly becoming obsolete. Our most basic instincts are for individual survival at any cost. Greed ensures that I will take what I need, at the expense of all others, while hatred provides the impetus to destroy anyone who threatens me or stands in my way. Both forms of desire create and support a sense of self, the one who must survive and reproduce no matter what.

The problem we now face is that these very instincts that have served us well in a primitive, competitive setting have become counterproductive in the interdependent social world we now inhabit and have themselves become our greatest existential threat. The greed and hatred that have kept us alive is now killing us. The adaptation required for human survival is thus an inner one—we must learn to reduce and even eliminate both the selfish greed driving the overconsumption of resources and the selfish hatred that so distains and despoils the living systems in which we are embedded.

Our vaunted human intelligence is little help in this matter, for it more often serves to further the ruination than to stop it. Even while intellect allows us to understand the harm we are causing, which can now be mapped out in some detail, it offers no useful solutions for how to stop. Delusion maintains a choking grip on our emotional intelligence. As primitive beings still, we simply do not have the self-knowledge to get ourselves out of the danger we are causing ourselves. Intellect tells us well enough what we are doing wrong, but it will take a much deeper intelligence to help us learn how to stop doing it.

This is where the Dharma comes in. It is a science of inner understanding and of inner adaptation. It teaches us that human suffering is self-created and that we can thus heal ourselves from our suffering by self-understanding, self-regulation, and self-transformation. In particular, the Dharma points to desire (both greed and hatred) as the cause of suffering and instructs us that any moment in which we are able to let go of desire will be a moment of greater well-being. Scaling this knowledge up from the personal to the collective realm, we gain a blueprint for survival: to whatever extent we are able as a species to diminish the impact of greed, hatred, and delusion upon our behaviors, we will thereby gain leverage over the forces threatening us.

The means for developing this ability to evolve beyond our current conditioning is wisdom, which is the antidote for the delusion sustaining greed and hatred. Wisdom is an inward-facing knowledge, and it must therefore be cultivated by the inner arts of meditation and experiential investigation. These have been woefully neglected in our modern civilization, which is more adept at effecting material alterations upon the outer world, but they have been well studied and preserved by ancient contemplative traditions. The time has come to learn the lessons offered by the inner sciences, and to use that knowledge to transform who we are and how we construct our world.

The Buddha appears to have demonstrated the next step in human evolution, wherein greed, hatred, and delusion can be entirely bypassed and expunged from the human psyche. He showed that these instincts, though deep, are not essential. As mammals we have also inherited a set of cooperative impulses that allow the expansion of one's perspective from *me* to *us*, from the merely personal to the family, pack, herd, or tribe. These traits encourage caring for others, and they render noble the impulse to regard one's own well-being as intertwined with the well-being of others.

At present both competitive and cooperative drives coinhabit our hearts, and scarcely a moment goes by when we are not called upon to feed one and starve the other. Choices are made, several times a second, that shape our actions. These will be either selfish actions that cause suffering to ourselves and others or selfless actions that help us get free of suffering. The thing is we can only make one choice at a time, so whenever we enact one, we neglect the other. Changing ourselves involves learning how to develop those states, behaviors, and dispositions that are healthy, while allowing the unhealthy ones to atrophy from neglect.

Our greatest ally in choosing the healthier path is the left prefrontal cortex, which is the region of the brain lighting up when one is mindful. Bringing heightened conscious awareness to bear dispels the darker forces of the more primitive mind, and doing so with equanimity provides access to all the innate healthier dispositions rooted in non-greed, non-hatred, and non-delusion.

Kindness, generosity, and wisdom can save us from ourselves. Our ancestors in India discovered this long ago and followed a noble path to the extinction of suffering. As this knowledge begins to permeate our current world view and show us a different course than the one we are on, we too can use the insights of introspection to tread a path away from extinction. It is time for us to evolve, or die trying.

A TREE CALLED STEADFAST

Once upon a time there was a royal fig tree called Steadfast, belonging to King Koravya, whose five outstretched branches provided a cool and pleasing shade. Its girth extended a hundred miles, and its roots spread out for forty miles. And the fruits of that tree were indeed great: as large as harvest baskets—such were its succulent fruits—and as clear as the honey of bees.

One portion was enjoyed by the king, along with his household of women; one portion was enjoyed by the army; one portion was enjoyed by the people of the town and village; one portion was enjoyed by sages and ascetics; and one portion was enjoyed by the beasts and birds. Nobody guarded the fruits of that royal tree, and neither did anyone harm one another for the sake of its fruits.

But then a certain man came along who fed upon as much of Steadfast's fruits as he wanted, broke off a branch, and wandered on his way. And the tree spirit, or *deva*, who dwelled in Steadfast thought to herself: "It is astonishing, it is truly amazing, that such an evil man would dare to feed upon as much of Steadfast's fruits as he wants, break off a branch, and then wander on his way! Now, what if Steadfast were in the future to bear no more fruit?" And so the royal fig tree Steadfast bore no more fruit.

So then King Koravya went up to where Sakka, chief among the gods, was dwelling, and having approached said this: "Surely you must know, sire, that Steadfast, the royal fig tree, no longer bears fruit?" And then Sakka created a magical creation such that a mighty wind and rain came down and toppled the royal fig tree Steadfast, uprooting it entirely. And then the deva who dwelled in Steadfast grieved, lamented, and stood weeping on one side with a face full of tears.

And then Sakka, chief among the gods, went up to where the deva was standing and having approached said this:

> "Why is it, deva, that you grieve and lament and stand on one side with a face full of tears?" "It is because, sire, a mighty wind and rain has come and toppled my abode, uprooting it entirely."
>
> "And were you, deva, upholding the dhamma of trees when this happened?" "But how is it, sire, that a tree upholds the dhamma of trees?"
>
> "Like this, deva: Root-cutters take the root of the tree; bark-strippers take the bark; leaf-pickers take the leaves; flower-pickers take the flowers; fruit-pickers take the fruits—and none of this is reason enough for a deva to think only of herself or become morose. Thus it is, deva, that a tree upholds the dhamma of trees." "Then indeed sire, I was not upholding the dhamma of trees when the mighty wind and rain came and toppled my abode, uprooting it entirely."
>
> "If it were the case, deva, that you were to uphold the dhamma of trees, it may be that your abode might be as it was before." "I will indeed, sire, uphold the dhamma of trees! May my abode be as it was before!"
>
> And then Sakka, chief among the gods, created a magical creation such that a mighty wind and rain came down and raised up the royal fig tree Steadfast, and its roots were entirely healed.[35]

Perhaps this is a true story—perhaps Steadfast is a name for the entire planet, not just a mythological tree. How else might we explain the earth's great forbearance and continued beneficence in the face of the rapacity and destruction we have wrought upon her? I think Gaia, the deity inhabiting the abode of our lovely Earth, was taught this lesson by Sakka in ancient times and has with great patience and dignity put up with the worst we can render. If this is true, then she will not give us a sign when we have gone too far—perceiving this to be our own responsibility.

Like every Buddhist story, this one works on many levels simultaneously. It is no accident that the great tree has five branches, or that the word used for each portion is *khandha*—the term designating the five psychophysical aggregates of form, feeling, perception, formations, and consciousness. The man eating his fill of fruit is manifesting greed, craving, or desire, and his breaking of the branch represents hatred, anger, or aversion. These are two of the three poisonous roots out of which all unwholesome action arises (the third—ignorance—is always present when the others occur). Thus the entire image is representative of a person being wronged by another or facing the eruption of their own latent tendencies for harmful action.

Notice that the story does not teach the evil man the folly of his ways, since there is often nothing one can do to avoid such people or such inclinations in oneself. The teaching is more about our *response* to transgression. Sakka's point is that it is self-centered to react petulantly to such an affront, and that the only suitable response is with kindness and generosity—to oneself as well as to others. As the *Dhammapada* so aptly says, "Never at any time in this world are hostilities resolved by hostility; but by kindness they are resolved—this has always been true."[36]

This teaching is given to Dhammika, a monk who complains of his treatment by certain laypeople. The Buddha reflects the situation back upon Dhammika, who as it turns out does not treat his fellow monks very well. It is an occasion to teach Dhammika, with the help of this story, the "dhamma of a recluse," which boils down to "not returning the insult of the insulter, the anger of the angry, or the abuse of the abuser." The healing has to begin somewhere.

SHINING A LIGHT

The Buddha offers more than a dozen convincing arguments against racism in a conversation with the Brahmins of his day who saw themselves as superior to others. These focus on the lack of any real biological or psychological distinction between people of different castes and point to social convention as the more obvious source of prejudice. You can read about this in the *Assalayana Sutta*,[37] but most people these days hardly need convincing of something so evident.

We do face the more challenging problem of how to uncover the socially constructed prejudices we all harbor and how to transform them, not at this level of intellectual argument but at the deeper level of changing emotional and behavioral responses. It is not about changing views (the aggregate of perception) but about reconstructing patterns of habitual reaction (the aggregate of formations). Fortunately the Buddha bequeathed us a powerful tool for doing this—mindfulness.

Psychology has demonstrated clearly that some of what we do is conscious, while much is unconscious. That is to say, we are consciously aware of a narrow band of our experience as it unfolds, but most of what happens is formulated out of view and emerges apparently on its own from the mysterious depths of the psyche to surge into behavior unhindered by awareness. Our views and reactions are formed as they appear, based on patterns laid down in the past, and consciousness is more a matter of observing what is already unfolding than of deciding what will take place next.

Mindfulness practice involves training the ability to observe what is happening within us in the present moment with an attitude of patience, kindness, and equanimity. As different bodily sensations or feeling tones or thoughts arise into conscious awareness, we watch along with (*anupassati*), or gaze evenly upon (*upekkhati*), or are simply aware of (*pajanati*) and fully experience (*patisamvedati*) them. If we get angry at what we see, or if any sort of response rooted in attraction or aversion occurs, then we are thrust out of mindful awareness and get carried away by an unhealthy emotional response. Eventually we may notice this is happening and return attention gently back to observing without judgment.

This is familiar territory to meditators. Now let's see how this might scale from the realm of internal personal experience to a collective, even global, practice of mindfulness. When something is caught on video and then digitally shared with a universal audience, this can be seen as bringing to conscious awareness what might otherwise remain unknown and unknowable to all but the immediate participants. The worldwide web is our collective mind, and the media sites that allow millions to see what one person has recorded can be regarded as supporting an emerging form of global meditation.

Witnessing an atrocity, observing injustice in action, or otherwise directly encountering the things that have historically been invisible is a way of shining the light of awareness into the dark corners of our world—much as meditation shines a light into the unexamined shadows of our mind. But the collective challenge is as daunting as the individual one: how do we bring patience, kindness, and equanimity to what we see instead of having it trigger and release the reservoirs of anger and hatred lurking within that are so ready and eager to erupt?

It is natural for fury to arise in the face of injustice, natural because our psyches are inhabited by primitive instincts adapted to survival at almost any cost. Anger is empowering, and conventional wisdom tells us that righteous anger is justified in such circumstances and is even necessary to move the mountains of discrimination, exploitation, and disrespect that perpetuate injustice. This may be true, but is it therefore the healthiest way to proceed? The Buddha was pointing us in a different direction. He encourages us to acknowledge such feelings but to then let go of them and respond instead with compassion and wisdom. Yes, laws and attitudes need to be changed, but how do we do that without doing further harm, or harming ourselves in the process?

The challenge and promise of mindfulness practice is not simply to become aware of things, but to do so with a particular attitude or emotional tone—a confident, benevolent, mindful, ethical, tranquil equanimity. When meditating, it does no good and some harm to blame yourself for your attention wandering off the breath, or to get annoyed at the person behind you for coughing, or to resent the fact that a pain is arising in your knee. In just the same way, it is not helpful and can make things worse to erupt in hatred toward the mob that stones an innocent woman, the officer that shoots an unarmed black man, or the fanatic who executes a helpless captive. The *object* of awareness may be reprehensible, but the *attitude* with which we are aware of it is a different matter and shapes who we are and what will happen next. All the great reformers (Gandhi, Mandela, King) knew the importance of this distinction and made it a cornerstone of their life's work.

One can know with *wisdom* that these acts are deeply wrong, feel unbounded *compassion* for the victims of the atrocity, conjure up the *energy* needed to see that the perpetrators are brought to justice, and work with *determination* and even *joy* to change the conditions enabling such transgressions to occur. These are healthy emotions and can be just as effective as their unhealthy counterparts. Taking this on as a practice, either when examining our own inner prejudices or exposing the injustices of the world, marks the difference between being swept along on the flood or working against the stream.

As the Buddha put it in some verses from the Connected Discourses:

> It is really a big mistake to return anger for anger.
> Not giving anger for anger, one wins a double victory.
> One behaves for the good of both: oneself and the other person.
> Knowing well the other's anger, one is mindful and remains calm.
> In this way one is healing both: oneself and the other person.
> The people who think "What a fool" just don't understand
>   the Dharma.[38]

7 Rethinking Buddhism

This world is blind! There are so few
who see things as they truly are.[39]
Come, take a good look at this world,
pretty like a king's chariot.[40]
Though fools become immersed in it,
for the wise there's no attachment.
Rouse yourself, and don't be lazy.
Follow the good ways of Dhamma.[41]

THE MINDFULNESS WEDGE

Mindfulness is the thin edge of a wedge that, if it wiggles its way deeply enough into our minds, will open them to wisdom. Whether or not this actually happens, however, depends on many things.

Some say the process is natural and inevitable, and once the practice of mindfulness is taken up its power of transformation is inexorable. This can sound similar to the monkeys-and-typewriters scenario though, and there is usually small print in the footnote invoking countless lifetimes over multiple eons. Most others acknowledge that mindfulness is a tool whose effectiveness requires such things as right view, diligent practice, long-term retreats, the guidance of a good teacher, a strong ethical base, and a karmic, if not genetic, predisposition for spiritual progress.

There is considerable enthusiasm for mindfulness these days, as long as it does not threaten to make us wise. Corporate tycoons would like to bring mindfulness into their world to help give them a competitive edge, as long as they do not have to spend too much of their valuable time meditating, and only if they can be reassured they will not lose their killer instincts and get all mushy and compassionate. And they are interested in training their workers in mindfulness, as long as it makes them more diligent and accepting of their duty, and does not raise troublesome ethical questions or throw them into a midlife crisis that leads them to drop out to do something more meaningful with their lives.

The same is true for the military, which is always interested in producing a more effective soldier. You have to be careful, though. There is the case of a man who quit his job as a police officer after getting involved with mindfulness meditation because he knew he would hesitate to shoot if he had to draw his weapon. This was a threat to his fellow officers, he knew, so he resigned. If this is the effect of mindfulness training, it clearly will not do for the armed forces. Yet we have seen how effective such training was for the samurai, and the ethical difficulties did not seem to intrude much at critical moments in the middle of the last century. Perhaps the wedge can be used to pry things open a little, without allowing the process to proceed too far.

When mindfulness is defined in contrast to mindlessness, it roughly means "attention," and this is the sense in which the word is most commonly used outside Buddhist circles these days. In an age when attention is a rare and precious commodity, even while it is spread around so promiscuously, training in attention skills is understandably popular. The ability to hold awareness upon a chosen object with some stability, or to return it to a primary object once it has strayed, and to do this without agitation, self-blame, or frustration, is a useful skill to learn. It is also the leading edge of the mindfulness wedge as described in the classical Buddhist texts.

But the crux of mindfulness training is found in the body of the wedge, the chorus that repeats sixteen times in the brief *Satipatthana Sutta*, the *Discourse on the Establishment of Mindfulness*: "One abides independent, not clinging to anything in the world." True mindfulness training involves learning to entirely disengage from, disidentify with, and become nonattached to the phenomena under review. Neither favoring nor opposing, neither liking nor disliking, "the Great Way is not difficult for one with no preferences" (to cite a later Chinese text). This disengagement is incompatible with corporate, military, and other secular applications of mindfulness training, however, since this is the very move that opens the way for wisdom.

The mind is habitually caught up in some very deep reflexes of craving and aversion. Wanting what pleases us and wanting to do away with what causes us distress is part of a primordial operating system that has served all creatures on this earth quite well for eons. Buddhism is pointing to an evolutionary step requiring us to abandon this reflex and replace it with a more mature mental state, equanimity. Classical mindfulness, unlike popular mindfulness, is all about the cultivation of equanimity. One is able to experience both pleasure *and* pain without clinging to anything in the world. One can be aware of what is gratifying *and* distressing, and still abide independent, not needing things to be other than they are.

According to the Buddhist analysis, reflexive craving and aversion keep us bound up with suffering. Any moment of desire is a moment of dissatisfaction, because desire, by definition, is an experience of lacking something. And the desire can never be satisfied, for even when our wishes are granted it is always in the next moment. Look for the truth of this in your own experience. Even when it feels like we get what we want, we immediately either worry it will slip away, yearn for more of it, or move on to wanting something else.

No amount of attention training is going to help us escape this cycle. In fact, incomplete mindfulness practice, focusing on attention but neglecting equanimity and the insights it brings, may serve only to strengthen the bonds that bind us. As the monk Nagasena tells King Menander when asked about this, "Goats, sheep, cows, buffaloes, camels, and donkeys have attention, but they do not have wisdom." He goes on to offer this analogy:

> As a barley-reaper grasps a handful of barley in the left hand
> and a sickle in the right and cuts it off with the sickle, even
> so does the earnest student, taking hold of the mind with
> attention, cut off the defilements with wisdom.[42]

Paying close attention to what is happening under our gaze is an important first step, but let's not get stuck with a handful of barley and our backsides pointed up in the air. Attending with an unattached attitude that allows us to understand the impermanent, interdependent, and selfless nature of it all is what is truly transformative. Not everyone is ready for such a transformation, so handle this tool with care.

WALKING THE TALK

In classical Buddhist teaching, meditation (*samādhi*) has always been sandwiched between integrity (*sīla*) on the one hand and wisdom (*paññā*) on the other. Indeed, this is what makes it Buddhist. As a technology for the attenuation of consciousness and the achievement of altered states of mind, meditation had been practiced by yogis for centuries before the Buddha, but in his hands it became a tool for the deep transformation of character that results in liberation of the mind from the toxins that cause suffering.

One might admire a craftsman's ability to sharpen a chisel to a fine edge, but surely the value of doing so lies in being able to then wield it skillfully as a tool, as well as in using it to create something worthwhile. This is also the case with meditation. Only if it is wielded skillfully, with integrity, can the benefits of a focused mind result in a noble outcome—a person who has quenched (or at least diminished) greed, hatred, and delusion through the development of wisdom.

What are we to think when we see people, many of them venerated teachers, who are highly skilled in meditation and yet demonstrate an appalling lack of integrity and thus an apparent lack of wisdom? One explanation sometimes offered is that people can be highly developed spiritually and yet underdeveloped emotionally. This is especially the case, the argument goes, for teachers who might have been raised in very traditional settings like a monastery and are then unleashed amid the wild freedoms of the secular world. I'm sorry, but I just don't buy it—even more so when the misbehavior is itself viewed as an expression of wisdom.

Moral integrity, concentration, and insight all grow together, conditioning one another every step of the way. Ethical mind states are a necessary precursor for meditation, because the mind is incapable of tranquility if agitated by the hindrances of sense desire, ill will, restlessness, sluggishness, and doubt. Ethical behavior is also the demonstrable result of wisdom, insofar as unwholesome states arise less often and with less intensity as wisdom deepens. Wisdom transforms the unconscious mind, rooting out impulses that lead to suffering for both oneself and others. It does this not by acting them out or suppressing them, but by the middle way of seeing clearly how impermanent they are, how ultimately unsatisfying they are, and how they are born in and nourished by the delusions of self. In short, one understands them, and thereby they lose their allure.

A more plausible explanation of teacher misbehavior is simply that they are demonstrating their lack of wisdom. Behavior is the outward expression of one's inner understanding, and only someone still firmly in the grip of craving and ignorance is capable of the heinous abuse of power, money, sexuality, and intoxication. Cultural forms being what they are, it can be difficult to distinguish the wisdom of the teacher from the wisdom of the teachings, especially for those unfamiliar with the profundities of Asian religious and philosophical tradition. Some very unwise people can say some very wise things. Much of Dharma teaching is a performance art, and it is easy to conflate the skill of the actor with the skill of the author.

The compilers of the early Buddhist texts seemed quite familiar with this dynamic. They urged judging a teacher first and foremost by the level of personal integrity they demonstrate:

> Are there in this teacher any states based on greed, hatred, or delusion such that, with his mind obsessed by those states, while not knowing, he might say, "I know," or while not seeing he might say "I see," or he might urge others to act in a way that would lead to their harm and suffering for a long time?[43]

Even a good teacher is capable of going wrong:

> How does a teacher's undoing come about? . . . He goes astray, becomes filled with desire, succumbs to craving, and reverts to luxury . . . He has been struck down by unwholesome states . . .[44]

But when wisdom has truly sunk in deep enough to be transformative, one is incapable of misbehavior:

> When a person . . . has understood that attachment is the root of suffering, and is without attachment . . . , it is not possible that he would direct his body or arouse his mind toward any object of attachment.[45]

Perhaps it is unfair to expect our teachers to be awakened. But it is not unreasonable for them to demonstrate some wakefulness from a lifetime of study and practice by managing to refrain from the mundane temptations that so easily corrupt an undeveloped mind. Many of them do, which make those who do not stand out so sorely. The primary seduction, of course, is selfhood, the insidious inclination toward conceit through which the teacher becomes more special than the teaching or the student's quest to embody it. Here too I think the Buddha was prescient when he said, just before passing away:

> What I have taught and explained to you as Dhamma and discipline will, at my passing, be your teacher.[46]

We are all walking a path together—some are a few steps ahead, some a few steps behind. Those behind will learn from the ones ahead, and those ahead will teach the ones who follow. We know where others are on this path not by what they say but by what they do. If their meditation prowess is not integrated with ethical behavior, which is the natural expression of a deep understanding, then they are just talking the talk.

CHERISH THE NUNS

After his awakening the Buddha made a return visit to his home town of Kapilavastu. An influential Sakyan chief (and cousin to Siddhartha) named Mahanama had the thought that, since many young men of good families had gone forth to join his growing monastic community, it would be good if some youths from the Buddha's own family joined also.

So before long a contingent of six Sakyan princes, including the well-known cousins Baddhiya, Anuruddha, Ananda, and Devadatta, snuck away from town and met up with the Buddha at a place called Anupiya. They were accompanied by their barber Upali, who was initially sent home with all their valuables, but who then decided that he too wanted to go forth into the life of the wandering mendicant. At this point the princes made a remarkable and generous gesture.

They knew that the Sangha of monks was organized entirely on a system of seniority, wherein people of all castes and all socioeconomic backgrounds would defer to one another solely on the basis of the order in which they joined the community. They addressed the Buddha, saying, "We, Lord, are Sakyans, we are proud. This barber has been our attendant for a long time. May the Lord let him go forth first. We will greet him, rise up before him, salute him with joined palms, and do the proper duties. Thus will the Sakyan pride be humbled in us Sakyans."

It was done as they wished, and Upali went on to become one of the most important members of the community, the one who memorized all the monastic laws and led the recitation of the Vinaya at the first council. It was a tribute to the Sakyan princes' integrity and commitment to the ideals of the movement that they were willing to humble themselves in this simple but highly symbolic way.

Some time later Pajapati, the Buddha's aunt and adoptive mother (taking over all maternal duties after the death in childbirth of her sister Maya), also asked to join the monastic community, which up to that time had monks but no nuns. The Buddha at first hesitated but then publically and officially said two very important things. When asked if women were capable of the same attainments as men, including complete awakening, if they practiced diligently, he declared clearly and without equivocation that they were. Soon after, in the proclamation founding the order of nuns, he made the formal statement "I allow nuns to be ordained by monks."

Pajapati and all the nuns who followed her had to agree to a set of special rules, and these had much to do with the protocols of respectful treatment between the two communities. Thus, for example, all monks have seniority over all nuns, and the order of ordination is reckoned separately within each group. Other rules ensured that the two communities were intertwined in much of their official functioning, but always preserving the priority and nominal seniority of the monks.

Over the years these special accommodations have been read differently by different groups. Some hold that the distinctions are minor and are not intended to disrespect the nuns but merely to integrate them into the Sangha in a way that was acceptable to the mores of ancient India. Others consider the symbolism enshrined in the disparity to be far from minor, and in light of the many ways one group has discriminated against another throughout history the discrepancy is a relic with no place in the modern expression of the Buddhist tradition.

The issue has come to the forefront in recent years, as the order of nuns is becoming reinstated after a breakdown of its continuity. Almost everyone involved recognizes that some changes need to be made, but considerable disagreement exists about how to go about making such changes and what the finished product should look like. As with every human movement, both religious and secular, there are conservatives, progressives, and every shade in between. How the issue is ultimately handled will reveal a lot about the nature of the people participating in the process, and it will inevitably demonstrate something important to all who look on about the values and customs of Buddhism itself.

Along these lines, I find myself wondering if we might all be inspired by the attitude of the Sakyan princes. Sooner or later, in one way or another, there will be monks and nuns living side by side in harmony, striving diligently to purify their minds of toxins and serving as an inspiration to all of us—as was the Buddha's original intention. What might it look like if, as a gesture of respect and conciliation, the monks requested that the seniority system be modified such that all nuns are considered senior to all monks?

If the effect of the distinction really is minor, then it will not greatly inconvenience the monks to assume a position of respect toward the nuns. And if the symbolism is significant it would send a powerful message to all, not only that the nuns are held in great esteem, but that the monks are gracious enough to make such an offer as an expression of their own wisdom. I cannot think of any essential Dharma teachings that would be disrupted by this gesture. And if the patriarchal systems of contemporary society are shaken up, then perhaps the karmic rebalancing that would ensue might contribute to greater overall health.

Every generation of Buddhists has faced the challenge of integrating what it understands as the core values of the tradition into a new and changing modern context, and each has no doubt faced its own set of daunting challenges. Might this not be an excellent opportunity to rise up to greet our sisters in the holy life, salute them with joined palms, and "let them go first"?

HELPING THE WORLD

The four noble truths formula is best known as one of the key insights gained by the Buddha on the night of his awakening, and it has become a ubiquitous schema for organizing and presenting his teachings. Most books on Buddhism include four chapters corresponding to suffering, its origin, its cessation, and the path leading to its cessation, and innumerable talks are organized along these lines as well.

It can also be regarded as a phenomenological device, guiding the meditator through a specific experiential landscape. The *Discourse on the Establishment of Mindfulness*[47] culminates with the phrase: "One is aware as it actually is, 'this is suffering . . . this is the arising of suffering . . . this is the cessation of suffering . . . this is the way leading to the cessation of suffering.'" In this context the formula is a meditative tool, a roadmap guiding one's insight into how experience is constructed and can be deconstructed, moment by moment.

I would like to suggest a third way the four truths formulation can be fruitfully used—as a template for social, economic, political, and environmental transformation. I imagine a four-part process of inquiry that can be implemented by any group of people, in any part of the world, under any circumstances. It might help to be guided through the process by a skilled facilitator, but I doubt this is strictly necessary. The method can be applied from the grassroots up, by local people with intimate knowledge of their own world and its own unique challenges.

The first step is to acknowledge suffering in all its manifestations by simply asking the question, "In what ways are people suffering here?" This is an exercise of naming what is actually happening, of cataloging symptoms clearly and empirically, of depicting the manifestations of suffering, without at this stage trying to link any of it to larger issues.

Perhaps these people are hungry or do not have access to clean water; or these people have no jobs; or these people have insufficient access to human rights or dignity; or these people are hated by those; or . . . the list in many cases will be very long.

The second step is to take that list and see to what extent specific causes can be identified for each of the instances of suffering. In one case it might be a lack of money; in another a corrupt official; or perhaps a cultural bias; or a recent environmental disaster; or a fundamentally unfair political system. The idea is to answer each item on the suffering list with a particular cause or set of causes. In some cases there will be a simple and local cause, in other cases there may be a long list of interrelated causes. But every instance of suffering will have a cause, and it may turn out that many forms of suffering are rooted in the same conditions.

The third part of the process is to go through the itemized causes of suffering and ask what solutions might present themselves for each. The questions in each case is "What has to change in order for this particular cause of this particular symptom of suffering to cease?" One will inevitably wind up investigating the multiple layers of interdependent conditions that shape and define any situation. At this stage the matter needs to be addressed theoretically rather than practically. Never mind whether a particular solution will work or not, just ask "What has to be different than it is for this to stop?" (You may recognize here the causal logic of interdependent origination used by the Buddha on the night of his awakening.)

The final phase is to go through all this work and sort out what can or cannot be done. There will surely be some things that are within reach and can be immediately addressed, even if these are very small things. Other matters will take more time and effort, but perhaps through this process a solution may at least come into sight. One thing tends to lead to another, and many destinations can only be reached by taking an oblique path. There will also be things on the list that will seem impossible. But by mapping out their causes, one may be able to begin taking very small steps in the general direction of their solution.

All change in nature is incremental, and according to Buddhist teachings all transformation is gradual. Patience and diligence are powerful tools for personal internal change, and they can be used just as effectively to bring about global external change. As the Buddha reminds us:

> There is work involving a small amount of activity, small function, small engagements, and small undertakings, which, when it succeeds, is of great fruit.[48]

Just as every mind is capable of liberation, regardless of its current state of affliction, I would like to think that the world, too, is capable of purification, despite every challenge, if only the right formula is applied.

Conclusion:
The Promise of Nonself

So hard it is to do, Lord,
It's so very hard to do.

But still they do what's hard to do,
Who steady themselves with virtue.[49]

We live in interesting times and are fortunate to witness the encounter between an irresistible force and an immovable object. The irresistible force is the Buddhist tradition, which has swept across Asia in past centuries and now stands ready to make an impact on the emerging global civilization. The immovable object is contemporary culture, rooted in centuries of European tradition, along with its lingering attitudes of intellectual ascendancy. Of particular interest is the encounter between the notion of selfhood, so central to modern thought, and the radical challenge to these assumptions posed by the Buddhist teachings of nonself. Nothing is so cherished in contemporary culture as the self, so much so that one might even say it acts as the organizing principle around which all contemporary culture is patterned. And nothing is quite as uniquely Buddhist as the critique of this idea.

Will mainstream thought succeed in resisting the Buddhist teachings of nonself, either directly, by answering and refuting the Buddhist articulation of the doctrine, or indirectly, by deflecting and co-opting these teachings to serve more subtly the purposes of self? Or will the popular assumptions of self be moved or even eradicated by the onslaught of the Buddhist critique, perhaps assisted by science, yielding a significantly different conception of the human condition on the part of non-Buddhist thinkers? My own opinion is that the former is well underway in the present and in the foreseeable future, but that the latter will eventually transpire. At the moment the Buddhist view of nonself is not well understood in popular culture, allowing its marginalization even by those who ostensibly take it to heart. But I think a number of emerging trends in the cognitive and neurological sciences are pointing the way to the eventual integration of the nonself perspective into new models of consciousness and, by inevitable implication, into broader psychological folk belief.

Two issues lie at the heart of these questions. The first has to do with how open the modern mind is to new ideas coming from beyond its historical cultural territory, and, in particular, to what extent intellectuals are capable of loosening their hold on their reflexive views of selfhood. The other issue has to do with how compelling the Buddhist notion of nonself really is. Is it indeed an insight of such subtlety that it managed to avoid the scrutiny of the world's best thinkers for centuries? Or does it turn out to be, upon closer investigation, something not particularly interesting or useful beyond the narrow agenda of Buddhist didactics? In other words, is it a profound and universal truth about the human condition, or just an intriguing artifact of ancient Indian thought?

The answer to such questions will only come from a careful investigation of the nonself teachings and will depend upon actually understanding what these are. Unfortunately there are several obstacles standing in the way of comprehending the Buddhist insight into nonself. Some of these are rooted in the limitations of language, and particularly in the languages used to express and understand Buddhist ideas. The structure of Indo-European languages, including both the Pali used to express the core teachings in the early texts and the English used to translate and interpret them today, are patterned around assumptions of agency and of subject/object relationship that do not easily yield alternative formulations.

Another obstacle is that Buddhist insights into the nature of self-view are built upon extensive empirical observation that is only available through the intensive practice of meditation and sustained attention to the textures of subjective experience. Such practices are not inherently unscientific, but they require a level of training that is rare in the contemporary world. But perhaps the most daunting obstacle is that, according to the Buddhist analysis of the issue, assumptions of self-identity are so deeply ingrained in the human psyche, and so powerfully distort the ability to see clearly, that direct insight into the nonself nature of existence is only attainable after a considerable degree of transformative individual work. Just as certain core insights of science, such as those described by Galileo, Darwin, and Einstein, are so thoroughly counterintuitive that many people even today do not accept them as true, so also the revelation of the insubstantial nature of identity is not easily seen or accepted by any but the most penetrating and open-minded thinkers.

The limitations of language

The limitations of language pose problems that are not easy to circumvent. Indo-European languages are largely built around nouns that take on modifiers and are subject to the action of verbs. This yields a habit of mind that is accustomed to construing the world as an edifice of persons, places, and things that exist, each with a defining essence, and to which can be attributed various qualities. But one of the key insights of Buddhist thought is that everything is so thoroughly in flux that only verbs can adequately signify dynamically arising and passing events. All nouns are an artificial construction of language, useful on conventional levels of discourse but inadequate as tools for looking closely at the nature of reality. As the nun Vajira famously says, "Just as for an arrangement of parts there occurs the word 'chariot', so also when there are aggregates there occurs the convention (*sammuti*) 'being.'"[50] The word used here for a conventional designation, *sammuti*, suggests a term that a number of people together (*sam-*) think ($\sqrt{man}$) carries an agreed-upon meaning. Nouns, in the Buddhist view, are a shared convention of language, which artificially create islands of meaning upon a constantly shifting sea of becoming. To say conventionally that something exists is merely an abbreviated way of saying that a dynamic process of arising and passing is occurring.

English, it has been said, is a language in which any noun can be verbed. We can do this with most static objects, even *table, chair, stone,* and *tree*. However the word for *self* seems to be uniquely resistant to this transformation and remains stubbornly a noun. There may be plenty of room for phenomenal flux in English, but what the word *self* is used to designate is the essence beneath these changes, the underlying structure, the deeper pattern, the primary complex—the concept that, by definition, projects stability and order where the Buddhists unremittingly say it is not naturally to be found. We have no acceptable way to say that one *selfed* yesterday, is *selfing* as we speak, but perhaps will try not *to self* as much next week. Any time we use *self* in a sentence, at least in English, we are forced into using it as an agent noun that is or is not, that does, feels, or thinks things, or that makes something happen. In short, self is a noun that cannot be verbed.

This is a substantial obstacle when it comes to trying to talk about, let alone understand, the Buddhist teachings about selfhood. If the English word *self* is thus thoroughly unsuited, and even incapable, of expressing the fundamentals of Buddhist psychology, then we should abandon it altogether and adopt nonself language. Any attempts to modify the word with adjectives, such as the "psychological self," the "conditional self," the "phenomenal self," or the "separate self," are likely to do more harm than good.

Refuted views of self

The notion of a self that the early Buddhists were challenging was based upon a number of assumptions and beliefs, each of which are carefully examined and contested in the early Buddhist texts. The existence of a soul was considered self-evident to the Shramana thinkers of the Buddha's day (Jains, Yogis, and others) and to those Brahmanical teachers who worked within the Upanishadic tradition. The arguments for the self challenged by the Buddhists included: *constancy*, the view that something unchanging underlies the perpetual flux of sensory and cognitive experience; *agency*, the felt sense of a person having the power to autonomously initiate action; *ownership*, the idea that all immediate experience was the intimate possession of a particular individual; *survival*, the widespread belief that an enduring personal pattern will be reborn after the break-up of the body; *responsibility*, the understanding that there must be a locus for the causal relations between a deed and its fruit; and *awareness*, the outlook that every individual is the center of a locally generated field of experience that is assumed to have sacred origins.

Constancy was challenged by an appeal to experience and by an analysis of the nature of consciousness. Whereas the Upanishads regularly suggest there is something behind or underlying the flux of sensory and mental phenomena, the Buddhists argue that a thorough examination of the phenomenal field, composed of the six sense spheres, the five aggregates, and the eighteen elements, will discover nothing exempt from the laws of change. Neither the organs nor the objects nor the act of cognition itself will ever arise and fall in the same way twice.

The Buddha presented himself as someone who had mastered to his utmost the available techniques of asceticism and meditation, and who had used these tools to fully explore the constructed world of experience.[51] It is from this perspective that he declared with great confidence that there was no essence, outside of or other than the field itself, that can be construed as an unchanging self. Moreover, having analyzed consciousness as a phenomenon emerging from the interaction of organs and objects of perception, he makes the argument that something dependent upon what is changeable cannot itself be exempt from changeability.[52] The Buddhist view is summed up by the well-known verse: "This body's like a ball of foam, and feeling is like a bubble; perception is like a mirage, formations like a pith-less tree, and consciousness is like a magician's trick; . . . no essence is discovered here."[53]

Agency was similarly considered to be an unwarranted assumption based upon an unexamined view of the workings of intention. It is true that there are times when it appears choices are freely made, but this is by no means a widespread phenomenon. The Buddha is said to have questioned Saccaka, "When you say 'The aggregates are my self,' do you exercise any such power over the aggregates as to say: 'Let my aggregates be thus; let my aggregates be not thus?'" "No, Master Gotama," Sacchaka has to concede.[54] It is one thing to be able to initiate some actions from time to time by the discretionary formulation of intention; it is another thing entirely to conclude from this that one is a free agent, operating outside the constraints of physical or mental cause and effect.

Exposing the fallacy of the agent noun is one of the principal insights of the early Buddhists. The Buddha himself is represented as consistently deflecting questions begging for an agent noun, and it is a significant advance of human thought to be able to recast such questions in nonpersonal language. For example when Moliya asks, "Who makes contact? . . . who feels? . . . who craves?" the Buddha is said to reply, "Not a valid question." The same matter should be more accurately put "With what as condition does contact . . . feeling . . . craving come to be?"[55] The teaching of dependent origination provides a model for the rigorous excerpting of personal language from a careful description of experience: "When this occurs that occurs; from the arising of this, that arises. When this does not occur, that does not occur; from the cessation of this, that ceases."

Ownership is also exposed as a projection of identity upon a process that is not inherently in anyone's possession. "This body is not yours," says the Buddha.

> These feelings, these perceptions, these dispositions, these [moments of] consciousness—are not yours.[56]

Therefore, whatever is not yours—abandon it! This will lead
to your welfare and happiness for a long time.[57]

These phrases articulate a remarkable observation from the phenomenological tradition of ancient India. They are not making a metaphysical statement about the nature of the mind and body; rather, they are
exposing a deeply held and largely unexamined psychological reflex.
Why is it that humans tend to feel possessive and acquisitive about all
aspects of their experience? The ownership of property is embedded in
most legal systems, but in drawing out the implications of the Buddhist
insight one sees that this is an extension of a much more pervasive habit
of mind. Moreover, it is this very sense of ownership that is directly
responsible for both individual and collective suffering. Ownership is a
node around which greed and hatred organize and is itself the expression of a fundamental delusion that gives rise to all sorts of strife. As the
matter is succinctly put in the *Dhammapada*:

"These sons are mine! This wealth is mine!" So are the mis-
informed incensed. But even their selves aren't their own—
let alone sons, let alone wealth.[58]

Survival is a matter of some nuance in Buddhist thought. The position of the early texts seems to be that patterns of character and karma
formation laid down in one lifetime serve to contribute to how experience is constructed in subsequent lifetimes. One might say, therefore,
along with Nagasena to King Milinda:

A continuity of dharmas is set up; one arises, another
ceases . . . and neither one nor the other can be reckoned the
last consciousness.[59]

But this is a far cry from the sort of personal survival and rebirth
proposed by those eternalists who see the soul as a spiritual energy undi-

minished by death. Again as Nagasena puts it, the one who arises in a new birth "is not the same and is not another" in relation to the person who passes away. Whatever hope is aroused by the prospect of the next person being not different from the last person is dashed by the fact that the reborn individual is also not the same. In other words even if rebirth occurs, this does not mean that *you* will survive *your* death. Indeed when the teachings of nonself settle thoroughly upon one's understanding, it is difficult to view a person even in the present life as maintaining some essential identity from moment to moment. When Sati said he understood rebirth to mean the running-on of personal consciousness he was rebuked by the Buddha:

> Misguided man, to whom have you ever known me to teach the Dhamma in that way? In many discourses have I not stated consciousness to be interdependently arisen?[60]

Responsibility is an important aspect of the Buddhist teachings around individual cause and effect, and a model is put forward that does not require the idea of a soul accumulating karmic formations. In a discussion with Kassapa, the Buddha cautions against the view of an unchanging agent: "The one who acts is the same as the one who experiences the result . . . this amounts to eternalism." But neither can it be said that there is no relationship: "The one who acts is one, the one who experiences the results is another . . . this amounts to annihilationism."[61]

The Buddha's middle teaching in this matter has to do with the principle of interdependent origination, wherein a complex interaction of impersonal events accounts for both continuity and change. The intentions of one moment alter one's dispositions, out of which the next moment's intentions will be molded. This allows for radical, though incremental, transformation of character, brought about by moment after moment of healthy rather than unhealthy action. In fact in the Buddhist model actions and their consequences take on somewhat more substantiality than the self. Karma is actual, while selfhood is illusory.

> Beings are heirs of their actions (*kamma*); they originate
> from their actions, are bound to their actions, and have their
> actions as their refuge. It is action that distinguishes beings
> as inferior and superior.[62]

Finally it is a widespread reflex of human thought that this node of *awareness* that yields the rich yet mysterious phenomenon of subjective, immediate experience must have sacred origins. Indeed there is nothing so intimate, nor so much a matter of ultimate concern, as the individual field of phenomenal awareness. The early Buddhists seem to understand and acknowledge this, but nevertheless caution against drawing unwarranted metaphysical conclusions on the basis of wishful thinking. In a discussion with a group of wise nuns, Nandaka points out the folly of investing substantial glory onto natural phenomena that are inherently dependent upon change. "Would anyone be speaking rightly who spoke thus: 'While this oil-lamp is burning, its oil, wick, and flame are impermanent and subject to change, but its radiance is permanent, everlasting, eternal, not subject to change'?" The nuns, of course, answer in the negative.[63] The early Buddhist texts weave together a way of understanding the human condition that is closer to modern scientific analysis than to religious impulses both ancient and modern. Nothing happens by chance, or by divine will. Everything happens because of a network of causes, and these causes can be discerned. In order to open to this way of looking at things, one has to both relinquish appeal to the authority of tradition and entertain a hearty skepticism as to how much can be "hammered out by reason."[64] The alternative to these two approaches involves careful empirical observation.

A phenomenal process

The Buddha appears to have been approaching the matter of the self from a radically phenomenological perspective. Using the ancient tools of asceticism, yoga, and meditation, he and many of his contemporaries were more interested in describing what is empirically observable in the mind and body than in theorizing from the abstract. As he put it in one of his discourses:

> It is in this fathom-long carcass, with its perceptions and thoughts, that the world (*loka*) arises and passes away.[65]

This way of looking at things involves a very different understanding of the word "world" than we are accustomed to, and it points the way to a different manner of construing "self." The word *loka* here refers not to the external world of rocks and trees (which can only manifest in direct experience as the conceptual handling of mental objects) but to the personal construction of a world of meaning in an individual psycho-physical organism. As Sariputta is said to have summarized the matter:

> Life, personhood, pleasure, and pain: this is all that's bound together in a single mental event—a moment that quickly takes place.[66]

The process language preferred by the Buddhism of the early textual tradition consists of spheres (*āyatana*) of sensory experience, groupings (*khandha*) of systemic functions, and patterns (*saṅkhāra*) of intention and disposition, all of which unfold together in mutual relationship (*paṭicca-samuppāda*), each moment (*khaṇika*), to shape (*kamma*) a world of individual experience (*loka*) that, because of certain habitual distortions of the mind (*vipallasa*), tends to be mistakenly (*avijjā*) viewed as consisting of a truly existing self (*sakkāya-diṭṭhi*). Rather than being the starting point of experience, the essential agent needed to *have* experience, self is regarded as the end product of an elaborate process of assimilating data, constructing meaning, and building a world of local experience. Rather than being an essential structure embedded in the heart of the psyche, self is regarded as a synthetic view that is fabricated every successive moment in the mind and body. Not only is the self as we cherish it unnecessary to the process, but it is considered by Buddhist tradition to be an erroneous, maladaptive, and downright hazardous invention of our instinctive human greed, hatred, and delusion.

The details of how to understand the fabrication of the view of self as an event rather than as a structure are found in the teachings of dependent origination. Consciousness emerges as a phenomenon—an arising and passing episode of awareness—when a sense organ and a sense object make contact. This moment of contact *consists* of the cognizing of a sensory object (forms, sounds, smells, tastes, or touches) or a mental object (thoughts, memories, plans, etc.) by means of a sensory organ (the eye, ear, nose, tongue, or body) or by means of the mental organ (mind). Also coarising with this cognition is a momentary perception that identifies the object in light of past experience and stored recognition patterns, along with a momentary feeling tone that knows the object as pleasant, unpleasant, or as carrying a feeling tone that is more neutral. When underlying tendencies of attachment, aversion, or confusion are enacted, craving toward (or away from) the object also arises. Craving manifests either as wanting pleasant feeling tones to persist (even as they inevitably pass away) or as wanting unpleasant sensations to go away (even as they continue to present at the sense door).

In the light of this disequilibrium between experience as it is manifesting and experience as one would want it to be, the mind and body naturally respond with an attitude the Buddhists call grasping or clinging (*upadāna*). Grasping is an intentional stance taken by the active response mechanisms of the psychophysical organism. It takes the form of either "attaching to" the object of the moment's experience or of "resisting" the object of experience. Whether it manifests as holding on or pushing away, the attitude of grasping creates an artificial distancing of "one's self" from what is happening in the moment. It is this grasping response that causes the becoming of self (*atta-bhāva*), the momentary birth and death of self-identity that inevitably involves suffering.

Self as a product of grasping

Viewed in this way, grasping is not something done by the self; rather, self is something done by grasping. To paraphrase how the matter is put in the *Discourse on the Simile of the Snake*, "Only when there is what belongs to a self is there a self."[67] It turns out that in the moment of trying to hold on to what is continually slipping away or of trying to push away what is relentlessly arising—the moment of grasping—a self is conjured up. The self can only exist as a fleeting attitude toward experience, one in which "the person who likes or does not like what is happening" is invented and defined.

And that person, so precisely delineated by its response to the moment's experience, like everything else constructed by the mind and body, vanishes as quickly as it is created. The very next moment the whole "world" of locally constructed experience is cobbled together again, and if the attitude of liking or not liking is re-created, then so too will another self be fashioned as an epiphenomenon of the perceptual process.

This kind of a self—self as an event, self as a response—arises and passes away as relentlessly as everything else. A virtual self is born and dies as fast as our senses are capable of constructing and relinquishing experience. When this happens repeatedly, the natural abilities of the mind to synthesize unity out of diversity and continuity out of discrete episodes of cognition conspire to create the illusion of a stable entity. Just as a series of still photos presented at high speed will be resolved by the mind into a continuous visual narrative, so also a succession of discrete "selves" will be identified in natural experience as the continuity of a single cohesive self. While each "moment of selfing" is actually grounded in a unique combination of coarising sense organ, sense object, consciousness, perception, and feeling, and is constructed by a unique intentional response to each moment, the patterns of such response demonstrated by any individual are both regular and idiosyncratic enough to yield the experience of a unique self. Recalling again the words of the wise nun Vajira, "In what is just a tangle of dispositions (*saṅkhāra*)—here a 'being' (*satta*) is not found."[68]

As the matter is explicated in the early Buddhist psychological literature, the construction of personality—the fashioning of a self—only occurs when an attitude of possession or appropriation takes place. Grasping merely consists of regarding any aspect of experience with the stance "This is mine; this is me; this is my self."[69] Contrary to popular belief, say the Buddhists, the *me* to which it all belongs does not actually pre-exist—it is created. When its moment passes away it is discarded, and another self is constructed to take temporary ownership of the next thing. Like a monkey swinging through the trees, consciousness grasps one object after another to create the stream of consciousness of felt experience. And like a burden clinging to the back of that monkey, the penchant to become a self (*atta-bhāva*), though ubiquitous, is not mandatory.

Reversing the process

The habit of routinely projecting the "view of a really existing person" (*sakkāya-diṭṭhi*) upon all aspects of experience is deeply ingrained, perhaps even instinctual. But it is simply, if not easily, reversed. One has only to replace the grasping response, the reflex of holding on or pushing away, with an attitude of "This is not mine, this is not me; this is not my self."[70] Since the view of a self is only created by *identification* with all aspects of experience—the objects of perception, the organs of perception, the act of cognizing the one with the other, the associated feeling tone, the corresponding perceptual icon, an emotional response—the view of self can be countered by systematically learning to *dis-identify* with the same field of experience.

How is this accomplished? It is a matter of holding oneself differently in the presence of every moment's experience. Nonself is more of an ongoing attitude than an alternative viewpoint. It involves participating consciously in the construction of sensory and cognitive experience, along with the texturing elements of perception and feeling, but not allowing the presence of pleasure or pain to give rise to liking or disliking the unfolding episode of experience. In short, overcoming the propensity to create a self who suffers each moment calls for replacing the habitual response of grasping with *equanimity*.

The Pali word for equanimity, *upekkha*, carries the sense of looking (√*iks*) upon (*upa-*) what is unfolding. That part of the mind responding to what is arising, the intentional stance required by each moment, becomes neutral or open rather than holding on or pushing away. Equanimity is not the sort of neutrality that disengages or becomes disinterested, but rather it is an open attitude that is capable of embracing either pleasure or pain without reflexively reacting to them. Being able to "look upon" pleasure without being seduced by it into the craving for more, or being able to "look upon" pain without pushing it away or craving for it to cease, involves a very different quality of response than what comes instinctively. The means for cultivating this quality is given in the meditation instructions of *Discourse on the Establishment of Mindfulness*: "One abides observing (*anupassin*) body as body, feeling as feeling, mind as mind, and mind objects as mind objects."[71] The word for observing used here has the sense of seeing (√*pas*) along with what is arising (*anu-*), of regarding what is unfolding without the interference of grasping.

In the actual practice of meditation one will find that the mind regularly intervenes on experience by liking or not liking, wanting or not wanting, but with patience and perseverance the new attitude of watching dispassionately can be cultivated and will gradually develop. At some point the meditator will be able to actually witness the process of self-creation as it unfolds. One learns to discern the differing texture of a moment's experience tinged with desire and a moment's experience held instead with equanimity. The former is always laced with some subtle sense of disequilibrium and dissatisfaction, while the latter is capable of a deep sense of well-being even in challenging circumstances. Access to the experience of well-being is regularly blocked by the construction of a self that holds on to or pushes away what is arising; but when the intervening sense of self is even temporarily abandoned through nongrasping or equanimity, then one can immediately access conscious experience that is naturally devoid of disturbances. The sense of this nonacquisitive abiding in the present moment is reflected in the verse: "What went before—let go of that! All that's to come—have none of it! Don't hold on to what's in between, and you'll wander fully at peace."[72]

Although such equanimity is often regarded as a "distancing" of oneself from experience, those who practice it regularly will soon discover that a far greater intimacy develops, calling for a good deal of courage, as the intervening concept of self is moved aside and experience is encountered more directly. When selfhood is constructed in any given moment of experience, one is not capable of engaging the full force of consciousness with the sensory or cognitive field. And when awareness is fully engaged with an object as it is, there is nothing left over with which a sense of self can be created. Put another way, when the senses are filled to their capacity by conscious awareness, one looses oneself. While this sounds threatening in principle, most people actually cherish the rare moments of heightened awareness that often accompany such a "loss of self."

Self as an option

One way to help understand what is happening each moment is to introduce the notion of consciousness and of selfhood as being parallel but asymmetrical transitive concepts. According to early Buddhist analysis, all conscious experience depends upon the inherent transitivity or intentionality of consciousness—one can only be aware *of* something. Whether seeing a form, hearing a sound, smelling an odor, tasting a flavor, touching a sensation, or thinking a thought, all forms of cognition involve the cognizing of an object. This insight points to the extent to which consciousness is an interactive process rather than an isolated and disembodied entity.

But contrary to the conventional wisdom, a subject is not automatically created along with the object. While *knowing* requires an object that is known, the *knowing of an object* does not necessitate an agent noun, a "knower." The subject only arises in a subsequent operation, when the act of consciousness is accompanied by some form of desire, of liking or wanting. Wanting is also an inherently transitive concept, but one that requires the creation of a subject rather than an object. For the notion of wanting to make any sense, there must be a *person who* enacts the episode of wanting. The object of that person's desire can be vague or even completely unknown, but wanting itself is a function of a person's inner intentional stance. This is demonstrated by the most common word used in the early teachings for desire, the word craving (*taṇhā*) which more elementally means *thirst*. Thirst describes a condition of disequilibrium experienced by a person. Whether they are thirsty for water, for alcohol, for justice, or for love is a secondary matter. The thirst can be triggered by the smell of water, for example, but the smelling of the odor is one thing and the wanting it for oneself is another.

So it is the nature of consciousness to create *objects* of experience using the sensory and cognitive organs (which are themselves nonpersonal or selfless) as a means of doing this. And it is the nature of desire to create *subjects* who arise through the establishment of a particular relationship to these objects of experience. A self is concocted as *the one who* likes or dislikes what is arising in consciousness, *the one who* accepts or rejects the content of the moment. And while a self can never develop without the construction of experience, enabled by the activity of consciousness, the reverse is not true: it is possible to have experience without the construction of a self. According to the Buddhist teachings, the self is abandoned whenever desire is abandoned, and consciousness, rather than disappearing, is thereby released from an unnecessary burden. The self is revealed as a secondary, almost parasitic, epiphenomenon to the human psychophysical system, bringing with it all manner of difficulty and suffering.

The awakening experienced by the Buddha under the Bodhi tree when he was thirty-six years old is described in the early Buddhist literature as cleansing the mind and body of its toxins—desire and ignorance. Greed, hatred, and delusion are primal instincts, and they probably have contributed much to the survival of both human and nonhuman species. But these root emotions have become maladaptive in the social and psychological realms humans now inhabit, and they are directly responsible for the manifestation of suffering. The Buddha is said to have discerned the subtle but profound truth that these qualities operate through instigating and reinforcing a view of self that sets itself off from what is arising and passing in experience. By shining the light of introspective awareness on the mechanism by which this occurs, one becomes empowered to reorder the process at any moment by replacing grasping with equanimity.

As the matter is stated in a poem attributed to the Buddha, "Seeing people locked in conflict, I became completely distraught. But then I discerned here a thorn—hard to see—lodged deep in the heart."[73] The thorn in the heart is desire, deeply embedded in human instinct that operates, through the construction of an illusory self, as an organizing principle around which all experience is ordered. The verse continues: "It's only when pierced by this thorn that one runs in all directions. So if that thorn is taken out—one does not run, and settles down."[74] With the recognition that the desiring self is the source of so many problems, the removal of this thorn will enable a profound healing of the mind and body.

The promise of nonself

The Buddhist doctrine of nonself is better seen as the practical antidote to a pernicious human problem than as an alternative metaphysical view. As the contemporary exploration of consciousness progresses, and as its mysteries are gradually revealed, the insights of ancient Buddhism become more relevant than ever. The postmodern view of the human condition is increasingly discovering the extent to which constructed experience is conditioned by interactive forces such as language, culture, and gender, and the neurosciences are ever more comprehensively mapping the coarising of subjective experience with electrochemical brain activity. As these movements progress, the received tradition regarding the soul is being inexorably run to ground. But just because we are compelled to give up on one extreme, the existence of a sacred and ineffable soul, does not mean we must simply embrace the other extreme, the reduction of human experience to its "merely" physical underpinnings. The middle way proposed by the Buddha encourages the abandoning of outdated and counterproductive superstitions, but it also invites getting far more intimately involved—moment after precious moment—with every instance of subjective experience.

I suspect that the Buddhist teaching of nonself will become increasingly important to the intellectual drama unfolding in the new sciences of consciousness and human potential, not because it is being proven "true," but because it offers a profound and meaningful outlook with which to fill the vacuum left by the loss of the soul. Something held as precious is very likely to be dislodged as the Buddhist view of nonself encounters the emerging contemporary understanding of mind and body, but it may turn out that something even more valuable will be discovered. The world of human experience may indeed be a virtual world, insofar as it is woven of sense spheres, aggregates, and moments of cognition. And while this might be ontologically disappointing, it can be phenomenologically liberating. The apparent need to *be someone* is viewed by Buddhist tradition as an unfortunate insecurity beyond which humanity is capable of evolving in a natural process of maturation. What replaces the imperative to forge an identity is an invitation to awaken to the full potential of conscious awareness. With the self out of the way, one is capable of ever more insightful mindfulness that opens to exploration of a vast and fascinating inner landscape.

Acknowledgments

Many pieces in this volume have been published singly in slightly different forms. I offer grateful acknowledgment to *Insight Journal, Tricycle, Shambhala Sun,* and *Buddhadharma* for having printed them originally.

Versions of the following pieces appeared in *Insight Journal,* the quarterly journal of the Barre Center for Buddhist Studies: "A Tree Called Steadfast" (Spring '97); "Cherish the Nuns" (Spring '10); "The Radical Buddha" (Winter '10); "A Protestant Buddhism" (Spring '11).

Versions of the following pieces appeared in *Tricycle: The Buddhist Review*: "I Think I Am" (Spring '10); "A Modest Awakening" (Summer '10); "The Other Dukkha" (Fall '10); "Mind Like a Mirror" (Winter '10); "A Perfect Storm" (Spring '11); "Blinded by Views" (Summer '11); "Castles Made of Sand" (Fall '11); "Deeper Health" (Spring '12); "Finding the Center" (Summer '12); "Pinch Yourself" (Fall '12); "The Buddha's Smile" (Winter '12); "Turning the Corner" (Spring '13); "Bait and Switch" (Summer '13); "Ten Billion Moments" (Fall '13); "The First Person" (Winter '13); "Pleasure and Pain" (Spring '14); "Simple Awareness" (Summer '14); "The Mindfulness Wedge" (Fall '14); "Waking Up" (Winter '14); "Growing Pains" (Spring '15); "Music of the Mind" (Summer '15); "Shining a Light" (Fall '15); and "Helping the World" (Winter '15).

Versions of the following appeared in *Shambhala Sun*: "Mind Comes First" (Winter '05); and "The Challenge of Nonself" (Fall '12).

A version of "Walking the Talk" appeared in *Buddhadharma* (May '13).

A version of the essay "The Promise of Nonself" first appeared in Nauriyal, et al., *Buddhist Thought and Applied Psychological Research* (New York: Routledge, 2006).

Notes

1. Samyutta Nikaya 1:23
2. Theragatha 517
3. Cullavagga 6:4.4
4. *Life of the Buddha*, translated by Patrick Olivelle (New York: New York University Press, 2008), 105–7.
5. Ibid. 127–29.
6. Ibid. 119.
7. Therigatha 118
8. Majjhima Nikaya 10
9. Anguttara Nikaya 1:6
10. Anguttara Nikaya 5:193
11. Majjhima Nikaya 19
12. Majjhima Nikaya 22
13. Majjhima Nikaya 148
14. Samyutta Nikaya 23:2
15. Samyutta Nikaya 23:2
16. Itivuttaka 3:7
17. Sutta Nipata 877
18. Gil Fronsdal. *The Dhammapada: A New Translation of the Buddhist Classic with Annotations* (Boston: Shambhala, 2006).
19. Majjhima Nikaya 117
20. Anguttara Nikaya 5:81
21. Samyutta Nikaya 46:12
22. Samyutta Nikaya 46:13
23. Samyutta Nikaya 47:19
24. Udana 6.4
25. Majjhima Nikaya 95
26. Mahaniddesa 1.42
27. Majjhima Nikaya 10
28. Abhidharma-sammuccaya 2.1.2
29. Dhammapada 154
30. Samyutta Nikaya 35:246
31. Visuddhimagga 20:97
32. Samyutta Nikaya 2:18
33. Samyutta Nikaya 36:6
34. Majjhima Nikaya 19
35. Anguttara Nikaya 6:5.54
36. Dhammapada 5
37. Majjhima Nikaya 93
38. Samyutta Nikaya 11:4
39. Dhammapada 174
40. Dhammapada 171
41. Dhammapada 168
42. Milindapanha 2.1.7–8
43. Majjhima Nikaya 95
44. Majjhima Nikaya 122
45. Majjhima Nikaya 105
46. Digha Nikaya 16
47. Majjhima Nikaya 10
48. Majjhima Nikaya 99
49. Samyutta Nikaya 2:6
50. Samyutta Nikaya 5:10
51. Majjhima Nikaya 111
52. Samyutta Nikaya 35:93
53. Samyutta Nikaya 22:95

54. Majjhima Nikaya 35

55. Samyutta Nikaya 12:12

56. Samyutta Nikaya 12:37

57. Majjhima Nikaya 22

58. Dhammapada 62

59. Milindapanha 40

60. Majjhima Nikaya 38

61. Samyutta Nikaya 12:15

62. Majjhima Nikaya 135

63. Majjhima Nikaya 146

64. Digha Nikaya 1

65. Anguttara Nikaya 4:45

66. Mahaniddesa 1.42

67. Majjhima Nikaya 22

68. Samyutta Nikaya 5:10

69. Majjhima Nikaya 148

70. Majjhima Nikaya 148

71. Majjhima Nikaya 10

72. Sutta Nipata 949

73. Sutta Nipata 938

74. Sutta Nipata 939

Index

Note: Page numbers followed by "q" indicate quotations.

About the Author

Andrew Olendzki is a Buddhist scholar, teacher, and writer living in Amherst, Massachusetts. Trained at Lancaster University (UK), the University of Sri Lanka (Perediniya), and Harvard, he was the first executive director at the Insight Meditation Society in Barre, MA, and went on to lead and teach at the Barre Center for Buddhist Studies for twenty-five years. He has also taught at numerous New England colleges (including Amherst, Brandeis, Connecticut, Hampshire, Harvard, Lesley, Montserrat, and Smith colleges), spent two years at the Mind & Life Institute heading up their Mapping the Mind project, and has been a longtime member of the Institute for Meditation and Psychotherapy. Andrew has contributed chapters to many books on Buddhist psychology, writes regularly for *Tricycle: The Buddhist Review*, and is the author of *Unlimiting Mind: The Radically Experiential Psychology of Buddhism* (Wisdom, 2010). He is currently creating and teaching a number of online courses as the senior scholar of the Integrated Dharma Institute.

What to Read Next from Wisdom Publications

Unlimiting Mind
The Radically Experiential Psychology of Buddhism
Andrew Olendzki

"This book has the power to change how you see yourself and the world. It's a remarkable read for anyone interested in the human condition."
—Christopher K. Germer, author of *The Mindful Path to Self-Compassion*

In the Buddha's Words
An Anthology of Discourses from the Pali Canon
Bhikkhu Bodhi
Foreword by His Holiness the Dalai Lama

"It will rapidly become the sourcebook of choice for both neophyte and serious student alike."—*Buddhadharma*

Buddhism
One Teacher, Many Traditions
His Holiness the Dalai Lama with Thubten Chodron
Foreword by Bhante Gunaratana

"This book will reward those who study it carefully with a deep and wide understanding of the way these traditions have mapped their respective visions of the path to enlightenment."—Bhikkhu Bodhi, translator of *In the Buddha's Words*

MindScience
An East-West Dialogue
His Holiness the Dalai Lama with Herbert Benson, Robert Thurman,
Howard Gardner, Daniel Goleman

"A lively and interesting description of the dynamic interaction between
Buddhism and mainstream science. Full of pearls."—*Lion's Roar*

Psychoanalysis and Buddhism
An Unfolding Dialogue
Edited by Jeremy Safran

"An extraordinary book. Safran deserves much praise."—Mark Epstein,
MD, author of *Thoughts without a Thinker*

About Wisdom Publications

Wisdom Publications is the leading publisher of classic and contemporary Buddhist books and practical works on mindfulness. To learn more about us or to explore our other books, please visit our website at wisdomexperience.org or contact us at the address below.

Wisdom Publications
199 Elm Street
Somerville, MA 02144 USA

We are a 501(c)(3) organization, and donations in support of our mission are tax deductible.

Wisdom Publications is affiliated with the Foundation for the Preservation of the Mahayana Tradition (FPMT).